THE PRAISE OF FOLLY

ERASMVS.

THE PRAISE OF FOLLY

DESIDERIUS ERASMUS

TRANSLATED BY JOHN WILSON

INTRODUCTION BY MICHAEL FRASSETTO

ILLUSTRATED WITH MANY CURIOUS CUTS,

DESIGNED, DRAWN, AND ETCHED

BY HANS HOLBEIN

BARNES & NOBLE

NEW YORK

THE BARNES & NOBLE
LIBRARY OF ESSENTIAL READING

Introduction and Suggested Reading
© 2004 by Barnes & Noble, Inc.

Originally published in 1511, revised 1522

This 2004 edition published by Barnes & Noble, Inc.

ISBN-13: 978-0-7607-5760-4
ISBN-10: 0-7607-5760-7

Printed and bound in the United States of America

3 5 7 9 10 8 6 4 2

CONTENTS

INTRODUCTION

THE PRAISE OF FOLLY, WRITTEN IN 1509 AND REVISED FOR PUBLICATION in 1511, is the most enduring and popular work of one of the greatest Renaissance humanists, Desiderius Erasmus of Rotterdam. Immensely popular in its own day, the work is a witty and often biting satire that offers an ironic appreciation of human vice and frivolity. *The Praise of Folly*, however, is not only an entertaining indictment of social mores, but also a moving declaration of Erasmus' Christian idealism, the philosophy of Christ. Although it is a product of the sixteenth century, *The Praise of Folly* remains to this day an insightful and relevant work of moral philosophy and social criticism.

Erasmus was born in an age of profound transformation and was a key figure in that period. His life spanned the Renaissance and Reformation, and his numerous writings provide important commentary on both movements. The greatest humanist of his day, Erasmus edited works of classical and Christian writers and prepared an important Greek edition of the New Testament. His literary works not only reflected the contemporary emphasis on elegant style but also indicted the church and its ministers. For this reason Erasmus was thought to have laid the egg that hatched Martin Luther. Many of the Protestant Reformers had first been followers of Erasmus, but he remained loyal to the church and rejected the ideas of Luther. Criticized by contemporary Catholics and Lutherans and some modern commentators for his actions during the Reformation, Erasmus nonetheless offered an alternative to the sectarian tumult that rocked his age and remains one of its most important representatives.

The second illegitimate son of a priest and of a doctor's daughter, Erasmus was born in Rotterdam around 1467. His parents died while

Erasmus was young, and he and his brother were placed under the guardianship of their schoolmaster. His early years were spent at Deventer, a school associated with the *devotio moderna*, a religious movement best known through *The Imitation of Christ* by Thomas à Kempis. After the death of his parents Erasmus had little choice but to join a monastery, where he began to reveal his literary talent. He also was given the opportunity to attend university; and although he found the lectures less than stimulating he advanced far enough to take on students of his own.

One of his students invited him to England, a momentous event in Erasmus' life. His first trip to England introduced him to several leading scholars and churchmen, notably the theologian John Colet and novelist Thomas More, who became his life-long friends. Erasmus' experience in England reinforced his own inclinations toward learning, inspired by Colet's exposition of Scripture. This would bear fruit when he returned to the Continent. Settling in the university town of Louvain, Erasmus published the *Enchiridion militis Christiani (Handbook of the Christian Soldier)*. This work provides a prelude to the core values of *The Praise of Folly* and Erasmus' Christian philosophy, which encouraged a moral piety that rejected the excesses that had crept into contemporary religious practices. In the previous year he had published the first edition of the *Adages*, a collection of Greek and Latin proverbs that signaled his deep interest in ancient letters and helped establish his reputation as a humanist scholar.

His fame growing, Erasmus rarely settled in one place, and his travels brought him into contact with many of the leading figures of his age. By the second decade of the sixteenth century, Erasmus' circle included leaders of church and state, and he himself was made a councilor of the emperor. He was offered an important position in the church by the pope, but he preferred not to hold any one position. Instead he sought the liberty to pursue the study of humane letters. A master of elegant Latin style and a student of the Greek language, Erasmus edited works of leading Latin and Greek authors, including Seneca, Lucian, and others. As his *Novum Testamentum*, his translation of the New Testament into Greek with accompanying Latin translation and commentary, indicates, his pursuit of letters was intended to improve and reform Christian belief and practice. Erasmus' studies introduced him to a wide range of authors and literary styles that laid the foundation for his most famous work.

In 1509, returning to England from a stay in Rome, Erasmus wrote *The Praise of Folly* or *Moriae encomium*, in honor of his friend Thomas More. The title is a play on the Greek word for praise, *moriae*, and the name of his friend More, who, Erasmus informs us, is far from a representative of folly. In fact, the book was dedicated to More, out of friendship and in recognition of the translations of Lucian he did with Erasmus. The work itself, Erasmus tells us, was written in only a week's time, and in 1522 Erasmus added a good bit of material to the original version. The original draft of the *Folly* was done while its author waited for the arrival of his books from Rome; he informs us though that even had they arrived he would have not been able to use them because a kidney illness prevented him from any serious study. The encomium was written merely to pass the time, its author tells us, but once begun Erasmus was encouraged by his friends to complete the work.

The book was an immense and immediate success despite Erasmus' comment that it was a mere trifle that he had not intended to publish. Among those who praised it were Pope Leo X and the humanists Jakob Wimpheling and Ulrich von Hutten, and its influence on European literature can be seen in the works of Rabelais, among others. The first edition of the book, written in Latin, was printed in Paris in June 1511. It was printed in Strasbourg in August of that year and again in 1512. There were further printings of the work in Paris and Antwerp in 1512. In 1515, a learned commentary was added to the edition printed in Basel, and the artist Hans Holbein the younger added illustrations that have appeared in numerous versions. There were some forty editions of the work published before Erasmus' death in 1536. *The Praise of Folly* was translated into French and German in 1520, into Italian in 1539, and into English in 1549. The work continued to be published after Erasmus' death and was well received by Enlightenment writers and by many in our own time, but despite its widespread popularity the work was not without its critics. Indeed, the conservative theologians at Louvain condemned it, and the critique of Martin Dorp prompted Erasmus to write a defense of his work. During the Reformation, the work was condemned by several popes and was placed on the index of forbidden books. Luther and a number of his followers also denounced the work for its alleged impiety.

Both widely popular and rather controversial in its day, *The Praise of Folly* was in many ways representative of its age. It was not the only critique of contemporary religion and society, preceded as it was by Sebastian Brant's *Ship of Fools*, and Erasmus' contemporaries clearly appreciated satire as the popularity of the anonymous *Julius Excluded from Heaven*, long attributed to Erasmus, and the work of von Hutton demonstrate. More than that, *The Praise of Folly* shares many of the basic values of the

Renaissance. Erasmus undertook the intensive study of Greek and Latin so that he could master the rhetorical and stylistic elegance expected of literary works of the day. Wisdom, it was thought, could best be conveyed through elegant literary style and language. And so *The Praise of Folly*, in ironic fashion, sought to speak wisely, and in the process it revealed the broad range of Erasmus' knowledge of classical literature. Like his contemporaries, Erasmus spread references to the writings of ancient Greek and Roman authors liberally throughout his encomium, and the book is shaped by the Neoplatonism so fashionable among circles of Renaissance humanists in Florence and elsewhere. There are direct references to or echoes of the works of such authors as Homer, Plato, Cicero, Virgil, and Seneca, among many others in *The Praise of Folly*, providing it with the wisdom of the ages and the authority of the ancients so important to contemporaries. The most important of the ancient authors for the writing of *The Praise of Folly* was the playwright Lucian, whose works, now mostly lost, provided the inspiration and model for Erasmus. But Erasmus, like Boccaccio perhaps, also drew from the vernacular and included a small number of Dutch proverbs in the eulogy given by the main character, the goddess Folly.

As the narrator, Folly offers a paradoxical and ironic encomium of herself and her followers, which, Erasmus notes in his prefatory letter, is much in the tradition of ancient letters. In her introductory remarks, Folly asserts that all creatures, mortal and immortal, are beholden to her and that without her life would lack joy and even a beginning. She boasts that she is the daughter of Plutus, the god of riches, who fathered her while he was young and hot-blooded, and that her nursemaids were the daughters of Bacchus, Drunkenness, and Pan, Ignorance. The oration that follows Folly's introduction of herself and her purpose, in which the paradoxical and satiric tone of the work is set, is divided into three sections in which she indulges first in the lighthearted praise of many human weaknesses and then proceeds along more biting lines. The second section, in which the voice of Erasmus appears at times most clearly, is a much harsher satire that condemns the more serious problems of the day. The social critiques of the middle part of the work thus prepared the way for the final section in which the narrator praises the folly of Jesus. *The Praise of Folly*, like the other works of Erasmus, was intended to promote a reformed Christian life.

The first major section of *The Praise of Folly*, which is the lightest and most humorous section of the work, lays the foundation for the ultimate conclusion, which is the praise of the folly of Christ. In passages that are timeless in their relevance, Folly extols the petty faults and the vanity of humankind. She praises elderly men and women who continue to act young, applying hair dyes and cosmetics in order to entice the attentions of the opposite sex. Not only elderly but all women are the followers of Folly because without the goddess what woman would endure the suffering of childbirth? Gamblers and fools belong to her, and, in a clear parody of himself, Erasmus has Folly claim scholars and wise men as her followers. Although the satire in this section is delivered in an almost comic fashion, its ironic praise of folly is clearly intended to honor wisdom and draw attention to the higher truths to follow.

The Praise of Folly then takes on a darker and bitterer tone, and Folly "praises" some of the most serious problems of the age. In this section, Folly, in a voice that is nearly that of Erasmus, turns her attention to the theologians, priests, and monks, who have so corrupted the church and brought it to the point of crisis. Folly "praises" the superstitious practices of many Christians, who indulge in the excesses of the saints' cults and other ritualized practices. She attacks indulgences and related abuses and emphasizes the importance of an internalized faith that is the cornerstone of his philosophy of Christ. She attacks the theologians in a long section in which she compares them with Paul and Peter and the other apostles. Unlike the theologians, the apostles were unlearned and were unskilled in the methods of dialectic and reason. The apostles lived a life of faith rooted in the teachings of Christ, whereas the theologians pay little attention to the Bible or the teachings of grace in favor of scholastic argument and the teachings of Aristotle and other theologians. And, in perhaps the harshest tones of the work, Folly denounces the violence and bloodshed caused by contemporary bishops and, especially, Pope Julius II, the "warrior pope." How, she wonders, can any Christian priest or layperson follow the true faith when the church's leaders live like courtiers and princes and indulge in ceremony and warfare?

Folly, aware of her harsh tone, makes light of her commentary on contemporary vice and once again assumes an ironic voice in the final section of the encomium. It is in this section, whose way was prepared by the first two, that the message of *The Praise of Folly* is revealed. She now praises the folly of the apostle Paul and, most important, that of Jesus. Citing passages from the Scriptures, the narrator points out the folly of Jesus, a fool who assumed the flesh to save the folly of humankind. The teachings of Christ, so distorted by the theologians and repudiated by the actions of the church hierarchy, are so clearly out of fashion with the practices of society and the customs praised earlier in Folly's oration. But, as the paradox established by Erasmus throughout the work implies, folly here is true wisdom. The simple life of faith advocated by Jesus and the apostles' ignorance and lack of guile praised as folly is the true path to salvation. The ways of Christ and the apostles that Folly mocks are, in the ironic tone of the work, what Erasmus is truly praising. The purpose of the *Moriae encomium* is both the praise of the simple Christian life, which is based on the Gospels and devoid of the superstitious practices that had crept in over the centuries, and the praise of learning in support of the Christian faith.

It is this simple message, reinforced in Folly's farewell to conclude the encomium, that retains its force to this day. A witty and elegant satire, *The Praise of Folly* calls on its readers to live the moral life in the face of the foolishness of everyday life. Behind its humorous façade, *The Praise of Folly* extols the simple moral life compiled in the Christian scriptures. Its message was lost in the generation following its publication when Europe was immersed in the turmoil of the Reformation and the wars of religion, but this message stands at the core of all of Erasmus' works. *The Praise of Folly* was possibly Erasmus' greatest contribution to his contemporaries, and Folly's ironic praise of the true path to wisdom remains an important lesson for us today.

Michael Frassetto is the religion editor at Encyclopaedia Britannica. He holds a Ph.D. in history from the University of Delaware, and he has taught at several colleges and written extensively on European religious and cultural history.

ERASMUS' EPISTLE
TO SIR THOMAS MORE

IN MY LATE TRAVELS FROM ITALY INTO ENGLAND, THAT I MIGHT NOT trifle away my time in the rehearsal of old wives' fables, I thought it more pertinent to employ my thoughts in reflecting upon some past studies, or calling to remembrance several of those highly learned, as well as smartly ingenious, friends I had here left behind, among whom you (dear SIR) were represented as the chief; whose memory, while absent at this distance, I respect with no less a complacency than I was wont while present to enjoy your more intimate conversation, which last afforded me the greatest satisfaction I could possibly hope for. Having therefore resolved to be a doing, and deeming that time improper for any serious concerns, I thought good to divert myself with drawing up a panegyrick upon Folly. How! What maggot (say you) put this in your head? Why, the first hint, Sir, was your own surname of More, which comes as near the literal sound of the word, as you yourself are distant from the signification of it, and that in all men's judgments is vastly wide. In the next place, I supposed that this kind of sporting wit would be by you more especially accepted of, by you, Sir, that are wont with this sort of jocose raillery (such as, if I mistake not, is neither dull nor impertinent) to be mightily pleased, and in your ordinary converse to approve yourself a Democritus junior: for truly, as you do from a singular vein of wit very much dissent from the common herd of mankind; so, by an incredible affability and pliableness of temper, you have the art of suiting your humour with all sorts of companies. I hope therefore you will not only readily accept of this rude essay as a token from your friend, but take it under your more immediate protection, as being dedicated to you, and by that title adopted for yours, rather than to be fathered as my own. And it is a chance if there be wanting some quarrelsome persons that will shew their teeth, and pretend these fooleries are either too buffoon-like for a grave divine, or too satyrical for a meek Christian, and so will exclaim against me as if I were vamping up some old farce, or acted anew the Lucian again with a peevish snarling at all things. But those who are offended at the lightness and pedantry of this subject, I would have them consider that I do not set myself for the first example of this kind, but that the same has been oft done by many considerable authors. For thus several ages since, Homer wrote of no more weighty a subject than of a war between the frogs and mice, Virgil of a gnat and a pudding-cake, and Ovid of a nut. Polycrates commended the cruelty of Busiris; and Isocrates, that corrects him for this, did as much for the injustice of Glaucus. Favorinus extolled Thersites, and wrote in praise of a quartan ague. Synesius pleaded in behalf of baldness; and Lucian defended a sipping fly. Seneca drollingly related the deifying of Claudius; Plutarch the dialogue betwixt Gryllus and Ulysses; Lucian and Apuleius the story of an ass; and somebody else records the last will of a hog, of which St. Hierom makes mention. So that if they please, let themselves think the worst of me, and fancy to themselves that I was all this while a playing at pushpin, or riding astride on a hobby-horse. For how unjust is it, if when we allow different recreations to each particular course of life, we afford no diversion to studies; especially when trifles may be a whet to more serious thoughts, and comical matters may be so treated of, as that a reader of ordinary sense may possibly thence reap more advantage than from some more big and stately argument: as while one in a long-winded oration descants in commendation of rhetoric or philosophy, another in a fulsome harangue sets forth the praise of his nation, a third makes a zealous invitation to a holy war with the Turks, another confidently sets up for a fortuneteller, and a fifth states questions upon mere impertinences. But as nothing is more childish than to handle a serious subject in a loose, wanton style, so is there nothing more pleasant than so to treat of trifles, as to make them seem nothing less than what their name imports. As to what relates to myself, I must be forced to submit to the judgment of others; yet, except I am too partial to be judge in my own case, I am apt to believe I have praised Folly in such a manner as not to have deserved the name of fool for my pains. To reply now to the objection of satyricalness, wits have been always allowed this privilege, that they might be smart upon any transactions of life, if so be their liberty did not extend to railing;

which makes me wonder at the tender-eared humour of this age, which will admit of no address without the prefatory repetition of all formal titles; nay, you may find some so preposterously devout, that they will sooner wink at the greatest affront against our Saviour, than be content that a prince, or a pope, should be nettled with the least joke or gird, especially in what relates to their ordinary customs. But he who so blames men's irregularities as to lash at no one particular person by name, does he (I say) seem to carp so properly as to teach and instruct? And if so, how am I concerned to make any farther excuse? Beside, he who in his strictures points indifferently at all, he seems not angry at one man, but at all vices.

Therefore, if any singly complain they are particularly reflected upon, they do but betray their own guilt, at least their cowardice. Saint Hierom dealt in the same argument at a much freer and sharper rate; nay, and he did not sometimes refrain from naming the persons: whereas I have not only stifled the mentioning any one person, but have so tempered my style, as the ingenious reader will easily perceive I aimed at diversion rather than satire. Neither did I so far imitate Juvenal, as to rake into the sink of vices to procure a laughter, rather than create a hearty abhorrence. If there be any one that after all remains yet unsatisfied, let him at least consider that there may be good use made of being reprehended by Folly, which since we have feigned as speaking, we must keep up that character which is suitable to the person introduced.

But why do I trouble you, Sir, with this needless apology, you that are so peculiar a patron; as, though the cause itself be none of the best, you can at least give it the best protection. Farewell.

ON THE ARGUMENT AND DESIGN OF THE FOLLOWING ORATION

Whate'er the modern satyrs o' th' stage,
To jerk the failures of a sliding age,
Have lavishly expos'd to public view,
For a discharge to all from envy due,
Here in as lively colours naked lie,
With equal wit, and more of modesty,
Those poets, with their free disclosing arts,
Strip vice so near to its uncomely parts,
Their libels prove but lessons, and they teach
Those very crimes which they intend t' impeach:
While here so wholesome all, tho' sharp t' th' taste,

So briskly free, yet so resolv'dly chaste;
The virgin naked as her god of bows,
May read or hear when blood at highest flows;
Nor more expense of blushes thence arise,
Than while the lect'ring matron does advise
To guard her virtue, and her honour prize.
   Satire and panegyric, distant be,
Yet jointly here they both in one agree.
The whole's a sacrifice of salt and fire;
So does the humour of the age require,
To chafe the touch, and so foment desire.
As doctrine-dangling preachers lull asleep
Their unattentive pent-up fold of sheep;
The opiated milk glues up the brain,
And th' babes of grace are in their cradles lain;
While mounted Andrews, bawdy, bold, and loud,
Like cocks, alarm all the drowsy crowd,
Whose glittering ears are prick'd as bolt-upright,
As sailing hairs are hoisted in a fright.
So does it fare with croaking spawns o' th' press,
The mould o' th' subject alters the success;
What's serious, like sleep, grants writs of ease,
Satire and ridicule can only please;
As if no other animals could gape,
But the biting badger, or the snick'ring ape.
   Folly by irony's commended here,
Sooth'd, that her weakness may the more appear.
Thus fools, who trick'd, in red and yellow shine,
Are made believe that they are wondrous fine,
When all's a plot t' expose them by design.
The largesses of Folly here are strown.
Like pebbles, not to pick, but trample on.
Thus Spartans laid their soaking slaves before
The boys, to justle, kick, and tumble o'er:
Not that the dry-lipp'd youngsters might combine
To taste and know the mystery of wine,
But wonder thus at men transform'd to swine;
And th' power of such enchantment to escape,

Timely renounce the devil of the grape.
   So here,
Though Folly speaker be, and argument,
Wit guides the tongue, wisdom's the lecture meant.

Erasmus' Praise of Folly

An oration, of feigned matter, spoken by FOLLY *in her own person*

HOW SLIGHTLY SOEVER I AM ESTEEMED IN THE COMMON VOGUE OF the world, (for I well know how disingenuously Folly is decried, even by those who are themselves the greatest fools), yet it is from my influence alone that the whole universe receives her ferment of mirth and jollity: of which this may be urged as a convincing argument, in that as soon as I appeared to speak before this numerous assembly all their countenances were gilded over with a lively sparkling pleasantness: you soon welcomed me with so encouraging a look, you spurred me on with so cheerful a hum, that truly in all appearance, you seem now flushed with a good dose of reviving nectar, when as just before you sate drowsy and melancholy, as if you were lately come out of some hermit's cell. But as it is usual, that as soon as the sun peeps from her eastern bed, and draws back the curtains of the darksome night; or as when, after a hard winter, the restorative spring breathes a more enlivening air, nature forthwith changes her apparel, and all things seem to renew their age; so at the first sight of me you all unmask, and appear in more lively colours. That therefore which expert orators can scarce effect by all their little artifice of eloquence, to wit, a raising the attentions of their auditors to a composedness of thought, this a bare look from me has commanded. The reason why I appear in this odd kind of garb, you shall soon be informed of, if for so short a while you will have but the patience to lend me an ear; yet not such a one as you are wont to hearken with to your reverend preachers, but as you listen withal to mountebanks, buffoons, and merry-andrews; in short, such as formerly were fastened to Midas, as a punishment for his affront to the god Pan. For I am now in a humour to act awhile the sophist, yet not of that sort who undertake the drudgery of tyrannizing over

1

schoolboys, and teach a more than womanish knack of brawling; but in imitation of those ancient ones, who to avoid the scandalous epithet of wise, preferred this title of sophists; the task of these was to celebrate the worth of gods and heroes. Prepare therefore to be entertained with a panegyrick, yet not upon Hercules, Solon, or any other grandee, but on myself, that is, upon Folly.

And here I value not their censure that pretend it is foppish and affected for any person to praise himself: yet let it be as silly as they please, if they will but allow it needful: and indeed what is more befitting than that Folly should be the trumpet of her own praise, and dance after her own pipe? For who can set me forth better than myself? Or who can pretend to be so well acquainted with my condition?

And yet farther, I may safely urge, that all this is no more than the same with what is done by several seemingly great and wise men, who with a new-fashioned modesty employ some paltry orator or scribbling poet, whom they bribe to flatter them with some high-flown character, that shall consist of mere lies and shams; and yet the persons thus extolled shall bristle up, and, peacock-like, bespread their plumes, while the impudent parasite magnifies the poor wretch to the skies, and proposes him as a complete pattern of all virtues, from each of which he is yet as far distant as heaven itself from hell: what is all this in the mean while, but the tricking up a daw in stolen feathers; a labouring to change the black-a-moor's hue, and the drawing on a pigmy's frock over the shoulders of a giant.

Lastly, I verify the old observation, that allows him a right of praising himself, who has nobody else to do it for him: for really, I cannot but admire at that ingratitude, shall I term it, or blockishness of mankind, who when they all willingly pay to me their utmost devoir, and freely acknowledge their respective obligations; that notwithstanding this, there should have been none so grateful or complaisant as to have bestowed on me a commendatory oration, especially when there have not been wanting such as at a great expense of sweat, and loss of sleep, have in elaborate speeches, given high encomiums to tyrants, agues, flies, baldness, and such like trumperies.

I shall entertain you with a hasty and unpremeditated, but so much the more natural discourse. My venting it *ex tempore*, I would not have you think proceeds from any principles of vain glory by which ordinary orators square their attempts, who (as it is easy to observe) when they are delivered of a speech that has been thirty years a conceiving, nay, perhaps at last, none of their own, yet they will swear they wrote it in a great

Folly readily receives Attention.

hurry, and upon very short warning: whereas the reason of my not being provided beforehand is only because it was always my humour constantly to speak that which lies uppermost. Next, let no one be so fond as to imagine, that I should so far stint my invention to the method of other pleaders, as first to define, and then divide my subject, i.e., myself. For it is equally hazardous to attempt the crowding her within the narrow limits of a definition, whose nature is of so diffusive an extent, or to mangle and disjoin that, to the adoration whereof all nations unitedly concur. Beside, to what purpose is it to lay down a definition for a faint resemblance, and mere shadow of me, while appearing here personally, you may view me at a more certain light? And if your eyesight fail not, you may at first blush discern me to be her whom the Greeks term Μωρία, the Latins *stultitia*.

But why need I have been so impertinent as to have told you this, as if my very looks did not sufficiently betray what I am; or supposing any be so credulous as to take me for some sage matron or goddess of wisdom, as if a single glance from me would not immediately correct their mistake, while my visage, the exact reflex of my soul, would supply and supersede the trouble of any other confessions: for I appear always in my natural colours, and an unartificial dress, and never let my face pretend one thing, and my heart conceal another; nay, and in all things I am so true to my principles, that I cannot be so much as counterfeited, even by those who challenge the name of wits, yet indeed are no better than jackanapes tricked up in gawdy clothes, and asses strutting in lions' skins; and how cunningly soever they carry it, their long ears appear, and betray what they are. These in troth are very rude and disingenuous, for while they apparently belong to my party, yet among the vulgar they are so ashamed of my relation, as to cast it in others' dish for a shame and reproach: wherefore since they are so eager to be accounted wise, when in truth they are extremely silly, what, if to give them their due, I dub them with the title of wise fools: and herein they copy after the example of some modern orators, who swell to that proportion of conceitedness, as to vaunt themselves for so many giants of eloquence, if with a double-tongued fluency they can plead indifferently for either side, and deem it a very doughty exploit if they can but interlard a Latin sentence with some Greek word, which for seeming garnish they crowd in at a venture; and rather than be at a stand for some cramp words, they will furnish up a long scroll of old obsolete terms out of some musty author, and foist them in, to amuse the reader with, that those who understand them may be tickled with the happiness of being acquainted with them: and those who understand them not, the less they know the more they may admire; whereas it has been always a custom to those of our side to contemn and undervalue whatever is strange and unusual, while those that are better conceited of themselves will nod and smile, and prick up their ears, that they may be thought easily to apprehend that, of which perhaps they do not understand one word. And so much for this; pardon the digression, now I return.

Of my name I have informed you, Sirs; what additional epithet to give you I know not, except you will be content with that of most foolish; for under what more proper appellation can the goddess Folly greet her devotees? But since there are few acquainted with my family and original, I will now give you some account of my extraction.

First then, my father was neither the chaos, nor hell, nor Saturn, nor Jupiter, nor any of those old, worn out, grandsire gods, but Plutus, the very same that, maugre Homer, Hesiod, nay, in spite of Jove himself, was the primary father of the universe; at whose alone beck, for all ages, religion and civil policy, have been successively undermined and re-established; by whose powerful influence war, peace, empire, debates, justice, magistracy, marriage, leagues, compacts, laws, arts, (I have almost run myself out of breath, but) in a word, all affairs of church and state, and business of private concern, are severally ordered and administered; without whose assistance all the Poets' gang of deities, nay, I may be so bold as to say the very major-domos of heaven, would either dwindle into nothing, or at least be confined to their respective homes without any ceremonies of devotional address: whoever he combats with as an enemy, nothing can be armour-proof against his assaults; and whosoever he sides with as a friend, may grapple at even hand with Jove, and all his bolts. Of such a father I may well brag; and he begot me, not of his brain, as Jupiter did the hag Pallas, but of a pretty young nymph, famed for wit no less than beauty: and this feat was not done amidst the embraces of dull nauseous wedlock, but what gave a greater gust to the pleasure, it was done at a stolen bout, as we may modestly phrase it. But to prevent your mistaking me, I would have you understand that my father was not that Plutus in Aristophanes, old, dry, withered, sapless and blind; but the same in his younger and brisker days, and when his veins were more impregnated, and the heat of his youth somewhat higher inflamed by a chirping cup of nectar, which for a whet to his lust he had just before drank very freely of at a merry-meeting of the gods. And now presuming

The Physician.

you may be inquisitive after my birthplace (the quality of the place we are born in, being now looked upon as a main ingredient of gentility), I was born neither in the floating Delo's, nor on the frothy sea, nor in any of these privacies, where too forward mothers are wont to retire for an undiscovered delivery; but in the fortune islands, where all things grow without the toil of husbandry, wherein there is no drudgery, no distempers, no old age, where in the fields grow no daffodills, mallows, onions, pease, beans, or such kind of trash, but there give equal divertisement to our sight and smelling, rue, all-heal, bugloss, marjoram, herb of life, roses, violets, hyacinth, and such like fragrances as perfume the gardens of Adonis. And being born amongst these delights, I did not, like other infants, come crying into the world, but perked up, and laughed immediately in my mother's face. And there is no reason I should envy Jove for having a she-goat to his nurse, since I was more creditably suckled by two jolly nymphs; the name of the first drunkenness, one of Bacchus' offspring, the other ignorance, the daughter of Pan; both which you may here behold among several others of my train and attendants, whose particular names, if you would fain know, I will give you in short. This, who goes with a mincing gait, and holds up her head so high, is Self-Love. She that looks so spruce, and makes such a noise and bustle, is Flattery. That other, which sits humdrum, as if she were half asleep, is called Forgetfulness. She that leans on her elbow, and sometimes yawningly stretches out her arms, is Laziness. This, that wears a plighted garland of flowers, and smells so perfumed, is Pleasure. The other, which appears in so smooth a skin, and pampered-up flesh, is Sensuality. She that stares so wildly, and rolls about her eyes, is Madness. As to those two gods whom you see playing among the lasses the name of the one is Intemperance, the other Sound Sleep. By the help and service of this retinue I bring all things under the verge of my power, lording it over the greatest kings and potentates.

You have now heard of my descent, my education, and my attendance; that I may not be taxed as presumptuous in borrowing the title of a goddess, I come now in the next place to acquaint you what obliging favours I everywhere bestow, and how largely my jurisdiction extends: for if, as one has ingenuously noted, to be a god is no other than to be a benefactor to mankind; and if they have been thought deservedly deified who have invented the use of wine, corn, or any other convenience for the well-being of mortals, why may not I justly bear the van among the

The Harp and the Ass.

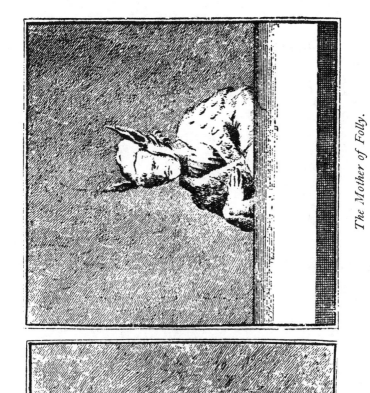

The Mother of Folly.

The Father of Folly.

The Wise Father and Foolish Son.

Jove and his Nurse.

whole troop of gods, who in all, and toward all, exert an unparalleled bounty and beneficence?

For instance, in the first place, what can be more dear and precious than life itself? And yet for this are none beholden, save to me alone. For it is neither the spear of thoroughly begotten Pallas, nor the buckler of cloud-gathering Jove, that multiplies and propagates mankind: but that prime father of the universe, who at a displeasing nod makes heaven itself to tremble, he (I say) must lay aside his frightful ensigns of majesty, and put away that grim aspect wherewith he makes the other gods to quake, and, stage player-like, must lay aside his usual character, if he would do that, the doing whereof he cannot refrain from, i.e., getting of children. The next place to the gods is challenged by the Stoicks; but give me one as stoical as ill-nature can make him, and if I do not prevail on him to part with his beard, that bush of wisdom, (though no other ornament than what nature in more ample manner has given to goats), yet at least he shall lay by his gravity, smooth up his brow, relinquish his rigid tenets, and in despite of prejudice become sensible of some passion in wanton sport and dallying. In a word, this dictator of wisdom shall be glad to take Folly for his diversion, if ever he would arrive to the honour of a father. And why should I not tell my story out? To proceed then: is it the head, the face, the breasts, the hands, the ears, or other more comely parts, that serve for instruments of generation? I trow not, but it is that member of our body which is so odd and uncouth as can scarce be mentioned without a smile. This part, I say, is that fountain of life, from which originally spring all things in a truer sense than from the elemental seminary. Add to this, what man would be so silly as to run his head into the collar of a matrimonial noose, if (as wise men are wont to do) he had beforehand duly considered the inconveniences of a wedded life? Or indeed what woman would open her arms to receive the embraces of a husband, if she did but forecast the pangs of childbirth, and the plague of being a nurse? Since then you owe your birth to the bride-bed, and (what was preparatory to that) the solemnizing of marriage to my waiting-woman Madness, you cannot but acknowledge how much you are indebted to me. Beside, those who had once dearly bought the experience of their folly, would never reengage themselves in the same entanglement by a second match, if it were not occasioned by the forgetfulness of past dangers. And Venus herself (whatever Lucretius pretends to the contrary), cannot deny, but that without my assistance, her procreative power would prove weak and ineffectual. It was from my sportive and tickling recreation that proceeded the old crabbed philosophers, and those who now supply their stead, the mortified monks and friars; as also kings, priests, and popes, nay, the whole tribe of poetic gods, who are at last grown so numerous, as in the camp of heaven (though ne'er so spacious), to jostle for elbow room. But it is not sufficient to have made it appear that I am the source and original of all life, except I likewise shew that all the benefits of life are equally at my disposal. And what are such? Why, can any one be said properly to live to whom pleasure is denied? You will give me your assent; for there is none I know among you so wise shall I say, or so silly, as to be of a contrary opinion. The Stoics indeed contemn, and pretend to banish pleasure; but this is only a dissembling trick, and a putting the vulgar out of conceit with it, that they may more quietly engross it to themselves: but I dare them now to confess what one stage of life is not melancholy, dull, tiresome, tedious, and uneasy, unless we spice it with pleasure, that hautgoust of Folly. Of the truth whereof the never enough to be commended Sophocles is sufficient authority, who gives me the highest character in that sentence of his,

To know nothing is the sweetest life.

Yet abating from this, let us examine the case more narrowly. Who knows not that the first scene of infancy is far the most pleasant and delightsome? What then is it in children that makes us so kiss, hug, and play with them, and that the bloodiest enemy can scarce have the heart to hurt them; but their ingredients of innocence and Folly, of which nature out of providence did purposely compound and blend their tender infancy, that by a frank return of pleasure they might make some sort of amends for their parents' trouble, and give in caution as it were for the discharge of a future education; the next advance from childhood is youth, and how favourably is this dealt with; how kind, courteous, and respectful are all to it? And how ready to become serviceable upon all occasions? And whence reaps it this happiness? Whence indeed, but from me only, by whose procurement it is furnished with little of wisdom, and so with the less of disquiet? And when once lads begin to grow up, and attempt to write man, their prettiness does then soon decay, their briskness flags, their humours stagnate, their jollity ceases, and their blood grows cold; and the farther they proceed in years, the more they grow backward in the enjoyment of themselves, till waspish old age comes on, a burden to itself as well as others, and that so heavy and oppressive, as none

The Birth of Folly.

King Solomon.

The Matrimonial Noose.

would bear the weight of, unless out of pity to their sufferings. I again intervene, and lend a helping-hand, assisting them at a dead lift, in the same method the poets feign their gods to succour dying men, by transforming them into new creatures, which I do by bringing them back, after they have one foot in the grave, to their infancy again; so as there is a great deal of truth couched in that old proverb, *Once an old man, and twice a child.* Now if any one be curious to understand what course I take to effect this alteration, my method is this: I bring them to my well of forgetfulness, (the fountain whereof is in the Fortunate Islands, and the river Lethe in hell but a small stream of it), and when they have there filled their bellies full, and washed down care, by the virtue and operation whereof they become young again. Ay, but (say you) they merely dote, and play the fool: why yes, this is what I mean by growing young again: for what else is it to be a child than to be a fool and an idiot? It is the being such that makes that age so acceptable: for who does not esteem it somewhat ominous to see a boy endowed with the discretion of a man, and therefore for the curbing of too forward parts we have a disparaging proverb, *Soon ripe, soon rotten?* And farther, who would keep company or have anything to do with such an old blade, as, after the wear and harrowing of so many years should yet continue of as clear a head and sound a judgment as he had at any time been in his middle-age; and therefore it is great kindness of me that old men grow fools, since it is hereby only that they are freed from such vexations as would torment them if they were more wise: they can drink briskly, bear up stoutly, and lightly pass over such infirmities, as a far stronger constitution could scarce master. Sometime, with the old fellow in Plautus, they are brought back to their horn-book again, to learn to spell their fortune in love. Most wretched would they needs be if they had but wit enough to be sensible of their hard condition; but by my assistance, they carry off all well, and to their respective friends approve themselves good, sociable, jolly companions. Thus Homer makes aged Nestor famed for a smooth oily tongued orator, while the delivery of Achilles was but rough, harsh, and hesitant; and the same poet elsewhere tells us of old men that sate on the walls, and spake with a great deal of flourish and elegance. And in this point indeed they surpass and outgo children, who are pretty forward in a softly, innocent prattle, but otherwise are too much tongue-tied, and want the other's most acceptable embellishment of a perpetual talkativeness. Add to this, that old men love to be playing with children, and children delight as much in them, to verify the proverb, that

The Schoolmaster.

Birds of a feather flock together. And indeed what difference can be discerned between them, but that the one is more furrowed with wrinkles, and has seen a little more of the world than the other? For otherwise their whitish hair, their want of teeth, their smallness of stature, their milk diet, their bald crowns, their prattling, their playing, their short memory, their heedlessness, and all their other endowments, exactly agree; and the more they advance in years, the nearer they come back to their cradle, till like children indeed, at last they depart the world, without any remorse at the loss of life, or sense of the pangs of death.

And now let any one compare the excellency of my metamorphosing power to that which Ovid attributes to the gods; their strange feats in some drunken passions we will omit for their credit sake, and instance only in such persons as they pretend great kindness for; these they transformed into trees, birds, insects, and sometimes serpents; but alas, their very change into somewhat else argues the destruction of what they were before; whereas I can restore the same numerical man to his pristine state of youth, health and strength; yea, what is more, if men would but so far consult their own interest, as to discard all thoughts of wisdom, and entirely resign themselves to my guidance and conduct, old age should be a paradox, and each man's years a perpetual spring. For look how your hard plodding students, by a close sedentary confinement to their books, grow mopish, pale, and meagre, as if, by a continual wrack of brains, and torture of invention, their veins were pumped dry, and their whole body squeezed sapless; whereas my followers are smooth, plump, and bucksome, and altogether as lusty as so many bacon-hogs, or sucking calves; never in their career of pleasure to be arrested with old age, if they could but keep themselves untainted from the contagiousness of wisdom, with the leprosy whereof, if at anytime they are infected, it is only for prevention, lest they should otherwise have been too happy.

For a more ample confirmation of the truth of what foregoes, it is on all sides confessed, that Folly is the best preservative of youth, and the most effectual antidote against age. And it is a never-failing observation made of the people of Brabant, that, contrary to the proverb of *Older and wiser,* the more ancient they grow, the more fools they are; and there is not any one country, whose inhabitants enjoy themselves better, and rub through the world with more ease and quiet. To these are nearly related, as well by affinity of customs, as of neighbourhood, my friends the Hollanders: mine I may well call them, for they stick so close and lovingly to me, that they are styled fools to a proverb, and yet scorn to be ashamed of their name. Well, let fond mortals go now in a needless quest of some Medea, Circe, Venus, or some enchanted fountain, for a restorative of age, whereas the accurate performance of this feat lies only within the ability of my art and skill.

It is I only who have the receipt of making that liquor wherewith Memnon's daughter lengthened out her grandfather's declining days: it is I that am that Venus, who so far restored the languishing Phaon, as to make Sappho fall deeply in love with his beauty. Mine are those herbs, mine those charms, that not only lure back swift time, when past and gone, but what is more to be admired, clip its wings, and prevent all farther flight. So then, if you will all agree to my verdict, that nothing is more desirable than the being young, nor any thing more loathed than contemptible old age, you must needs acknowledge it as an unrequitable obligation from me, for fencing off the one, and perpetuating the other.

But why should I confine my discourse to the narrow subject of mankind only? View the whole heaven itself, and then tell me what one of that divine tribe would not be mean and despicable, if my name did not lend him some respect and authority. Why is Bacchus always painted as a young man, but only because he is freakish, drunk, and mad; and spending his time in toping, dancing, masking, and revelling, seems to have nothing in the least to do with wisdom? Nay, so far is he from the affectation of being accounted wise, that he is content, all the rights of devotion which are paid unto him should consist of apishness and drollery. Farther, what scoffs and jeers did not the old comedians throw upon him? *O swinish punch-gut god*, say they, *that smells rank of the sty he was sowed up in*, and so on. But prithee, who in this case, always merry, youthful, soaked in wine, and drowned in pleasure, who, I say, in such a case, would change conditions, either with the lofty menace-looking Jove, the grave, yet timorous Pan, the stately Pallas, or indeed any one other of heaven's landlords? Why is Cupid feigned as a boy, but only because he is an under-witted whipster, that neither acts nor thinks any thing with discretion? Why is Venus adored for the mirror of beauty, but only because she and I claim kindred, she being of the same complexion with my father Plutus, and therefore called by Homer the Golden Goddess? Beside, she imitates me in being always a laughing, if either we believe the poets, or their near kinsmen the painters, the first mentioning, the other drawing her constantly in that posture. Add farther, to what deity did the Romans pay a more ceremonial respect than to Flora, that bawd of obscenity? And if any one search the poets for an historical account

Suspicion.

Momos Thrust out of Heaven.

Scribes and Pharisees.

of the gods, he shall find them all famous for lewd pranks and debaucheries. It is needless to insist upon the miscarriages of others, when the lecherous intrigues of Jove himself are so notorious, and when the pretendedly chaste Diana so oft uncloaked her modesty to run a hunting after her beloved Endimion. But I will say no more, for I had rather they should be told of their faults by Momus, who was want formerly to sting them with some close reflections, till nettled by his abusive raillery, they kicked him out of heaven for his sauciness of daring to reprove such as were beyond correction: and now in his banishment from heaven he finds but cold entertainment here on earth, nay, is denied all admittance into the court of princes, where notwithstanding my handmaid Flattery finds a most encouraging welcome: but this petulant monitor being thrust out of doors, the gods can now more freely rant and revel, and take their whole swinge of pleasure. Now the beastly Priapus may recreate himself without contradiction in lust and filthiness; now the sly Mercury may, without discovery, go on in his thieveries, and nimble-fingered juggles; the sooty Vulcan may now renew his wonted custom of making the other gods laugh by his hopping so limpingly, and coming off with so many dry jokes, and biting repartees. Silenus, the old doting lover, to shew his activity, may now dance a frisking jig, and the nymphs be at the same sport naked. The goatish satyrs may make up a merry ball, and Pan, the blind harper may put up his bagpipes, and sing bawdy catches, to which the gods, especially when they are almost drunk, shall give a most profound attention. But why would I any farther rip open and expose the weakness of the gods, a weakness so childish and absurd, that no man can at the same time keep his countenance, and make a relation of it? Now therefore, like Homer's wandering muse, I will take my leave of heaven, and come down again here below, where we shall find nothing happy, nay, nothing tolerable, without my presence and assistance. And in the first place consider how providently nature has took care that in all her works there should be some piquant smack and relish of Folly: for since the Stoics define wisdom to be conducted by reason, and folly nothing else but the being hurried by passion, lest our life should otherwise have been too dull and inactive, that creator, who out of clay first tempered and made us up, put into the composition of our humanity more than a pound of passions to an ounce of reason; and reason he confined within the narrow cells of the brain, whereas he left passions the whole body to range in. Farther, he set up two sturdy champions to stand perpetually on the guard, that reason might make no assault, surprise, nor in-road: anger,

More Votaries of Folly.

Silenus, Pan, and the Satyr.

which keeps its station in the fortress of the heart; and lust, which like the signs Virgo and Scorpio, rules the belly and secret members. Against the forces of these two warriors how unable is reason to bear up and withstand, every day's experience does abundantly witness; while let reason be never so importunate in urging and reinforcing her admonitions to virtue, yet the passions bear all before them, and by the least offer of curb or restraint grow but more imperious, till reason itself, for quietness sake, is forced to desist from all further remonstrance.

But because it seemed expedient that man, who was born for the transaction of business, should have so much wisdom as should fit and capacitate him for the discharge of his duty herein, and yet lest such a measure as is requisite for this purpose might prove too dangerous and fatal, I was advised with for an antidote, who prescribed this infallible receipt of taking a wife, a creature so harmless and silly, and yet so useful and convenient, as might mollify and make pliable the stiffness and morose humour of man. Now that which made Plato doubt under what genus to rank woman, whether among brutes or rational creatures, was only meant to denote the extreme stupidness and Folly of that sex, a sex so unalterably simple, that for any of them to thrust forward, and reach at the name of wise, is but to make themselves the more remarkable fools, such an endeavour, being but a swimming against the stream, nay, the turning the course of nature, the bare attempting whereof is as extravagant as the effecting of it is impossible: for as it is a trite proverb, *That an ape will be an ape, though clad in purple;* so a woman will be a woman, i.e., a fool, whatever disguise she takes up. And yet there is no reason women should take it amiss to be thus charged; for if they do but rightly consider they will find it is to Folly they are beholden for those endowments, wherein they so far surpass and excel man; as first, for their unparalleled beauty, by the charm whereof they tyrannize over the greatest tyrants; for what is it but too great a smatch of wisdom that makes men so tawny and thick-skinned, so rough and prickly bearded, like an emblem of winter or old age, while women have such dainty smooth cheeks, such a low gentle voice, and so pure a complexion, as if nature had drawn them for a standing pattern of all symmetry and comeliness? Beside, what greater or juster aim and ambition have they than to please their husbands? In order whereunto they garnish themselves with paint, washes, curls, perfumes, and all other mysteries of ornament; yet after all they become acceptable to them only for their Folly. Wives are always allowed their humour, yet it is only in exchange for titillation and pleasure, which indeed are but other names for Folly; as none can deny, who consider how a man must hug, and dandle, and kittle, and play a hundred little tricks with his bed-fellow when he is disposed to make that use of her that nature designed her for. Well, then, you see whence that greatest pleasure (to which modesty scarce allows a name), springs and proceeds.

But now some blood-chilled old men, that are more for wine than wenching, will pretend, that in their opinion the greatest happiness consists in feasting and drinking. Grant it be so; yet certainly in the most luxurious entertainments it is Folly must give the sauce and relish to the daintiest cates and delicacies; so that if there be no one of the guests naturally fool enough to be played upon by the rest, they must procure some comical buffoon, that by his jokes, and flouts, and blunders shall make the whole company split themselves with laughing: for to what purpose were it to be stuffed and crammed with so many dainty bits, savoury dishes, and toothsome rarities, if after all this epicurism of the belly, the eyes, the ears, and the whole mind of man, were not as well foistred and relieved with laughing, jesting, and such like divertisements, which like second courses serve for the promoting of digestion? And as to all those shooing horns of drunkenness, the keeping every one his man, the throwing hey-jinks, the filling of bumpers, the drinking two in a hand, the beginning of mistress' healths; and then the roaring out of drunken catches, the calling in a fiddler, the leading out every one his lady to dance, and such like riotous pastimes, these were not taught or dictated by any of the wise men of Greece, but of Gotham rather, being my invention, and by me prescribed as the best preservative of health: each of which, the more ridiculous it is, the more welcome it finds. And indeed to jog sleepingly through the world, in a dumpish melancholy posture cannot properly be said to live, but to be wound up as it were in a winding-sheet before we are dead, and so to be shuffled quick into a grave, and buried alive.

But there are yet others perhaps that have no gust in this sort of pleasure, but place their greatest content in the enjoyment of friends, telling us that true friendship is to be preferred before all other acquirements; that it is a thing so useful and necessary, as the very elements could not long subsist without a natural combination; so pleasant that it affords as warm an influence as the sun itself; so honest, (if honesty in this case deserve any consideration), that the very philosophers have not stuck to place this as one among the rest of their different sentiments of the chiefest good. But what if I make it appear that I also am the main spring and original of this

Youth and Old Age—the Matrimonial Chain.

The Logician.

endearment? Yes, I can easily demonstrate it, and that not by crabbed syllogisms, or a crooked and unintelligible way of arguing, but can make it (as the proverb goes) *As plain as the nose on your face.* Well then, to scratch and curry one another, to wink at a friend's faults; nay, to cry up some failings for virtuous and commendable, is not this the next door to the being a fool? When one looking stedfastly in his mistress' face, admires a mole as much as a beauty spot; when another swears his lady's stinking breath is a most redolent perfume; and at another time the fond parent hugs the squint-eyed child, and pretends it is rather a becoming glance and winning aspect than any blemish of the eyesight, what is all this but the very height of Folly? Folly (I say) that both makes friends and keeps them so. I speak of mortal men only, among whom there are none but have some small faults; he is most happy that has fewest. If we pass to the gods, we shall find that they have so much of wisdom, as they have very little of friendship; nay, nothing of that which is true and hearty. The reason why men make a greater improvement in this virtue, is only because they are more credulous and easy natured; for friends must be of the same humour and inclinations too, or else the league of amity, though made with never so many protestations, will be soon broke. Thus grave and morose men seldom prove fast friends; they are too captious and censorious, and will not bear with one another's infirmities; they are as eagle sighted as may be in the espial of others' faults, while they wink upon themselves, and never mind the beam in their own eyes. In short, man being by nature so prone to frailties, so humoursome and cross-grained, and guilty of so many slips and miscarriages, there could be no firm friendship contracted, except there be such an allowance made for each other's defaults, which the Greeks term 'Εvήθεια, and we may construe good nature, which is but another word for Folly. And what? Is not Cupid, that first father of all relation, is not he stark blind, that as he cannot himself distinguish of colours, so he would make us as mope-eyed in judging falsely of all love concerns, and wheedle us into a thinking that we are always in the right? Thus every Jack sticks to his own Jill; every tinker esteems his own trull; and the hobnailed suiter prefers Joan the milkmaid before any of my lady's daughters. These things are true, and are ordinarily laughed at, and yet, however ridiculous they seem, it is hence only that all societies receive their cement and consolidation.

The same which has been said of friendship is much more applicable to a state of marriage, which is but the highest advance and improvement

The Plague of being a Nurse.

of friendship in the closest bond of union. Good God! What frequent divorces, or worse mischief, would oft sadly happen, except man and wife, were so discreet as to pass over light occasions of quarrel with laughing, jesting, dissembling, and such like playing the fool? Nay, how few matches would go forward, if the hasty lover did but first know how many little tricks of lust and wantonness (and perhaps more gross failings) his coy and seemingly bashful mistress had oft before been guilty of? And how fewer marriages, when consummated, would continue happy, if the husband were not either sottishly insensible of, or did not purposely wink at and pass over the lightness and forwardness of his good-natured wife? This peace and quietness is owing to my management, for there would otherwise be continual jars, and broils, and mad doings, if want of wit only did not at the same time make a contented cuckold and a still house; if the cuckoo sing at the back door, the unthinking cornute takes no notice of the unlucky omen of others' eggs being laid in his own nest, but laughs it over, kisses his dear spouse, and all is well. And indeed it is much better patiently to be such a henpecked frigot, than always to be wracked and tortured with the grating surmises of suspicion and jealousy. In fine, there is no one society, no one relation men stand in, would be comfortable, or indeed tolerable, without my assistance; there could be no right understanding betwixt prince and people, lord and servant, tutor and pupil, friend and friend, man and wife, buyer and seller, or any persons however otherwise related, if they did not cowardly put up small abuses, sneakingly cringe and submit, or after all fawningly scratch and flatter each other. This you will say is much, but you shall yet hear what is more; tell me then, can any one love another that first hates himself? Is it likely any one should agree with a friend that is first fallen out with his own judgment? Or is it probable he should be any way pleasing to another, who is a perpetual plague and trouble to himself? This is such a paradox that none can be so mad as to maintain. Well, but if I am excluded and barred out, every man would be so far from being able to bear with others, that he would be burthensome to himself, and consequently incapable of any ease or satisfaction. Nature, that toward some of her products plays the stepmother rather than the indulgent parent, has endowed some men with that unhappy peevishness of disposition, as to nauseate and dislike whatever is their own, and much admire what belongs to other persons, so as they cannot in any wise enjoy what their birth or fortunes have bestowed upon them: for what grace is there in the greatest beauty, if it be always clouded with frowns and sulliness? Or what vigour in youth, if it be harassed with a pettish, dogged, waspish, ill humour? None, sure. Nor indeed can there be any creditable acquirement of ourselves in any one station of life, but we should sink without rescue into misery and despair, if we were not buoyed up and supported by self-love, which is but the elder sister (as it were) of Folly, and her own constant friend and assistant. For what is or can be more silly than to be lovers and admirers of ourselves? And yet if it were not so there will be no relish to any of our words or actions. Take away this one property of a fool, and the orator shall become as dumb and silent as the pulpit he stands in; the musician shall hang up his untouched instruments on the wall; the completest actors shall be hissed off the stage; the poet shall be burlesqued with his own doggrel rhymes; the painter shall himself vanish into an imaginary landscape; and the physician shall want food more than his patients do physic. In short, without self-love, instead of beautiful, you shall think yourself an old beldam of fourscore; instead of youthful, you shall seem just dropping into the grave; instead of eloquent, a mere stammerer; and in lieu of gentle and complaisant, you shall appear like a downright country clown; it being so necessary that every one should think well of himself before he can expect the good opinion of others. Finally, when it is the main and essential part of happiness to desire to be no other than what we already are; this expedient is again wholly owing to self-love, which so flushes men with a good conceit of their own, that no one repents of his shape, of his wit, of his education, or of his country; so as the dirty half-drowned Hollander would not remove into the pleasant plains of Italy, the rude Thracian would not change his boggy soil for the best seat in Athens, nor the brutish Scythian quit his thorny deserts to become an inhabitant of the Fortunate Islands. And oh the incomparable contrivance of nature, who has ordered all things in so even a method that wherever she has been less bountiful in her gifts, there she makes it up with a larger dose of self-love, which supplies the former defects, and makes all even. To enlarge farther, I may well presume to aver, that there are no considerable exploits performed, no useful arts invented, but what I am the respective author and manager of: as first, what is more lofty and heroical than war? And yet, what is more foolish than for some petty, trivial affront, to take such a revenge as both sides shall be sure to be losers, and where the quarrel must be decided at the price of so many limbs and lives? And when they come to an engagement, what service can be done by such pale-faced students, as by drudging at the oars of wisdom, have spent all their strength and activity? No, the only use is of blunt sturdy fellows that

The Fool in the Family.

have little of wit, and so the more of resolution; except you would make a soldier of such another Demosthenes as threw down his arms when he came within sight of the enemy, and lost that credit in the camp which he gained in the pulpit. But counsel, deliberation, and advice (say you), are very necessary for the management of war: very true, but not such counsel as shall be prescribed by the strict rules of wisdom and justice; for a battle shall be more successfully fought by serving-men, porters, bailiffs, padders, rogues, gaol-birds, and such like tag-rags of mankind, than by the most accomplished philosophers; which last, how unhappy they are in the management of such concerns, Socrates (by the oracle adjudged to be the wisest of mortals) is a notable example; who when he appeared in the attempt of some public performance before the people, he faltered in the first onset, and could never recover himself, but was hooted and hissed home again: yet this philosopher was the less a fool, for refusing the appellation of wise, and not accepting the oracle's compliment; as also for advising that no philosophers should have any hand in the government of the commonwealth; he should have likewise at the same time, added, that they should be banished all human society. And what made this great man poison himself to prevent the malice of his accusers? What made him the instrument of his own death, but only his excessiveness of wisdom? Whereby, while he was searching into the nature of clouds, while he was plodding and contemplating upon ideas, while he was exercising his geometry upon the measure of a flea, and diving into the recesses of nature, for an account how little insects, when they were so small, could make so great a buzz and hum; while he was intent upon these fooleries he minded nothing of the world, or its ordinary concerns.

Next to Socrates comes his scholar Plato, a famous orator indeed, that could be so dashed out of countenance by an illiterate rabble, as to demur, and hawk, and hesitate, before he could get to the end of one short sentence. Theophrastus was such another coward, who beginning to make an oration, was presently struck down with fear, as if he had seen some ghost, or hobgoblin. Isocrates was so bashful and timorous, that though he taught rhetoric, yet he could never have the confidence to speak in public. Cicero, the master of Roman eloquence, was wont to begin his speeches with a low, quivering voice, just like a schoolboy, afraid of not saying his lesson perfect enough to escape whipping: and yet Fabius commends this property of Tully as an argument of a considerate orator, sensible of the difficulty of acquitting himself with credit: but what hereby does he do more than plainly confess that wisdom is but a rub and impediment to the well management of any affair? How would these heroes crouch, and shrink into nothing, at the sight of drawn swords, that are thus quashed and stunned at the delivery of bare words?

Now then let Plato's fine sentence be cried up, that "happy are those commonwealths where either philosophers are elected kings, or kings turn philosophers." Alas, this is so far from being true, that if we consult all historians for an account of past ages, we shall find no princes more weak, nor any people more slavish and wretched, than where the administrations of affairs fell on the shoulders of some learned bookish governor. Of the truth whereof, the two Catos are exemplary instances: the first of which embroiled the city, and tired out the senate by his tedious harangues of defending himself, and accusing others; the younger was an unhappy occasion of the loss of the peoples' liberty, while by improper methods he pretended to maintain it. To these may be added Brutus, Cassius, the two Gracchi, and Cicero himself, who was no less fatal to Rome, than his parallel Demosthenes was to Athens: as likewise Marcus Antoninus, whom we may allow to have been a good emperor, yet the less such for his being a philosopher; and certainly he did not do half that kindness to his empire by his own prudent management of affairs, as he did mischief by leaving such a degenerate successor as his son Commodus proved to be; but it is a common observation, that *A wise father has many times a foolish son*, nature so contriving it, lest the taint of wisdom, like hereditary distempers, should otherwise descend by propagation. Thus Tully's son Marcus, though bred at Athens, proved but a dull, insipid soul; and Socrates his children had (as one ingeniously expresses it) "more of the mother than the father," a phrase for their being fools. However, it were the more excusable, though wise men are so awkward and unhandy in the ordering of public affairs, if they were not so bad, or worse in the management of their ordinary and domestic concerns; but alas, here they are much to seek: for place a formal wise man at a feast, and he shall, either by his morose silence put the whole table out of humour, or by his frivolous questions disoblige and tire out all that sit near him. Call him out to dance, and he shall move no more nimbly than a camel: invite him to any public performance, and by his very looks he shall damp the mirth of all the spectators, and at last be forced, like Cato, to leave the theatre, because he cannot unstarch his gravity, nor put on a more pleasant countenance. If he engage in any discourse, he either breaks off abruptly, or tires out the patience of the whole company, if he goes on: if he have any

Personifying a Prince.

contract, sale, or purchase to make, or any other worldly business to trans-
act, he behaves himself more like a senseless stock than a rational man;
so as he can be of no use nor advantage to himself, to his friends, or to
his country; because he knows nothing how the world goes, and is wholly
unacquainted with the humour of the vulgar, who cannot but hate a
person so disagreeing in temper from themselves.

And indeed the whole proceedings of the world are nothing but one
continued scene of Folly, all the actors being equally fools and madmen;
and therefore if any be so pragmatically wise as to be singular, he must
even turn a second Timon, or man-hater, and by retiring into some
unfrequented desert, become a recluse from all mankind.

But to return to what I first proposed, what was it in the infancy of the
world that made men, naturally savage, unite into civil societies, but only
flattery, one of my chiefest virtues? For there is nothing else meant by
the fables of Amphion and Orpheus with their harps; the first making the
stones jump into a well-built wall, the other inducing the trees to pull their
legs out of the ground, and dance the morrice after him. What was it that
quieted and appeased the Roman people, when they brake out into a riot
for the redress of grievances? Was it any sinewy starched oration? No,
alas, it was only a silly, ridiculous story, told by Menenius Agrippa, how the
other members of the body quarrelled with the belly, resolving no longer
to continue her drudging caterers, till by the penance they thought thus
in revenge to impose, they soon found their own strength so far dimin-
ished, that paying the cost of experiencing a mistake, they willingly returned
to their respective duties. Thus when the rabble of Athens murmured
at the exaction of the magistrates, Themistocles satisfied them with such
another tale of the fox and the hedgehog; the first whereof being stuck
fast in a miry bog, the flies came swarming about him, and almost sucked
out all his blood, the latter officiously offers his service to drive them away;
no, says the fox, if these which are almost glutted be frighted off, there will
come a new hungry set that will be ten times more greedy and devouring:
the moral of this he meant applicable to the people, who if they had such
magistrates removed as they complained of for extortion, yet their successors would certainly be worse.

With what highest advances of policy could Sertorius have kept
the Barbarians so well in awe, as by a white hart, which he pretended was
presented to him by Diana, and brought him intelligence of all his enemies' designs? What was Lycurgus his grand argument for demonstrating

the force of education, but only the bringing out two whelps of the same bitch, differently brought up, and placing before them a dish, and a live hare; the one, that had been bred to hunting, ran after the game; while the other, whose kennel had been a kitchen, presently fell a licking the platter. Thus the before-mentioned Sertorius made his soldiers sensible that wit and contrivance would do more than bare strength, by setting a couple of men to the plucking off two horses' tails; the first pulling at all in one handful, tugged in vain; while the other, though much the weaker, snatching off one by one, soon performed his appointed task.

Instances of like nature are Minos and king Numa, both which fooled the people into obedience by a mere cheat and juggle; the first by pretending he was advised by Jupiter, the latter by making the vulgar believe he had the goddess Ægeria assistant to him in all debates and transactions. And indeed it is by such wheedles that the common people are best gulled and imposed upon.

For farther, what city would ever submit to the rigorous laws of Plato, to the severe injunctions of Aristotle? Or the more unpracticable tenets of Socrates? No, these would have been too straight and galling, there not being allowance enough made for the infirmities of the people.

To pass to another head, what was it made the Decii so forward to offer themselves up as a sacrifice for an atonement to the angry gods, to rescue and stipulate for their indebted country? What made Curtius, on a like occasion, so desperately to throw away his life, but only vainglory, that is condemned, and unanimously voted for a main branch of Folly by all wise men? What is more unreasonable and foppish (say they) than for any man, out of ambition to some office, to bow, to scrape and cringe to the gaping rabble, to purchase their favour by bribes and donatives, to have their names cried up in the streets, to be carried about as it were for a fine sight upon the shoulders of the crowd, to have their effigies carved in brass, and put up in the market place for a monument of their popularity? Add to this, the affectation of new titles and distinctive badges of honour; nay, the very deifying of such as were the most bloody tyrants. These are so extremely ridiculous, that there is need of more than one Democritus to laugh at them. And yet hence only have been occasioned those memorable achievements of heroes, that have so much employed the pens of many laborious writers.

It is Folly that, in a several dress, governs cities, appoints magistrates, and supports judicatures; and, in short, makes the whole course of man's life a mere children's play, and worse than pushpin diversion. The invention of all arts and sciences are likewise owing to the same cause: for what sedentary, thoughtful men would have beat their brains in the search of new and unheard-of-mysteries, if not egged on by the bubbling hopes of credit and reputation? They think a little glittering flash of vainglory is a sufficient reward for all their sweat, and toil, and tedious drudgery, while they that are supposedly more foolish, reap advantage of the others' labours.

And now since I have made good my title to valour and industry, what if I challenge an equal share of wisdom? How! This (you will say) is absurd and contradictory; the east and west may as soon shake hands as Folly and Wisdom be reconciled. Well, but have a little patience and I will warrant you I will make out my claim. First then, if wisdom (as must be confessed) is no more than a readiness of doing good, and an expedite method of becoming serviceable to the world, to whom does this virtue more properly belong? To the wise man, who partly out of modesty, partly out of cowardice, can proceed resolutely in no attempt; or to the fool, that goes hand over head, leaps before he looks, and so ventures through the most hazardous undertaking without any sense or prospect of danger? In the undertaking any enterprize the wise man shall run to consult with his books, and daze himself with poring upon musty authors, while the dispatchful fool shall rush bluntly on, and have done the business, while the other is thinking of it. For the two greatest lets and impediments to the issue of any performance are modesty, which casts a mist before men's eyes; and fear, which makes them shrink back, and recede from any proposal: both these are banished and cashiered by Folly, and in their stead such a habit of fool-hardiness introduced, as mightily contributes to the success of all enterprizes. Farther, if you will have wisdom taken in the other sense, of being a right judgment of things, you shall see how short wise men fall of it in this acceptation.

First, then, it is certain that all things, like so many Janus', carry a double face, or rather bear a false aspect, most things being really in themselves far different from what they are in appearance to others: so as that which at first blush proves alive, is in truth dead; and that again which appears as dead, at a nearer view proves to be alive: beautiful seems ugly, wealthy poor, scandalous is thought creditable, prosperous passes for unlucky, friendly for what is most opposite, and innocent for what is hurtful and pernicious. In short, if we change the tables, all things are found placed in a quite different posture from what just before they appeared to stand in.

If this seem too darkly and unintelligibly expressed, I will explain it by the familiar instance of some great king or prince, whom everyone shall suppose to swim in a luxury of wealth, and to be a powerful lord and master; when, alas, on the one hand he has poverty of spirit enough to make him a mere beggar, and on the other side he is worse than a galley-slave to his own lusts and passions.

If I had a mind farther to expatiate, I could enlarge upon several instances of like nature, but this one may at present suffice.

Well, but what is the meaning (will some say) of all this? Why, observe the application. If anyone in a playhouse be so impertinent and rude as to rifle the actors of their borrowed clothes, make them lay down the character assumed, and force them to return to their naked selves, would not such a one wholly discompose and spoil the entertainment? And would he not deserve to be hissed and thrown stones at till the pragmatical fool could learn better manners? For by such a disturbance the whole scene will be altered: such as acted the men will perhaps appear to be women: he that was dressed up for a young brisk lover, will be found a rough old fellow; and he that represented a king, will remain but a mean ordinary serving-man. The laying things thus open is marring all the sport, which consists only in counterfeit and disguise. Now the world is nothing else but such another comedy, where everyone in the tire-room is first habited suitably to the part he is to act; and as it is successively their turn, out they come on the stage, where he that now personates a prince, shall in another part of the same play alter his dress, and become a beggar, all things being in a mask and particular disguise, or otherwise the play could never be presented. Now if there should arise any starched, formal don, that would point at the several actors, and tell how this, that seems a petty god, is in truth worse than a brute, being made captive to the tyranny of passion; that the other, who bears the character of a king, is indeed the most slavish of serving-men, in being subject to the mastership of lust and sensuality; that a third, who vaunts so much of his pedigree, is no better than a bastard for degenerating from virtue, which ought to be of greatest consideration in heraldry, and so shall go on in exposing all the rest; would not anyone think such a person quite frantic, and ripe for bedlam? For as nothing is more silly than preposterous wisdom, so is there nothing more indiscreet than an unreasonable reproof. And therefore he is to be hooted out of all society that will not be pliable, conformable, and willing to suit his humour with other men's, remembering the law of clubs and meetings, that he who will not do as the rest must get him out of the company. And it is certainly one great degree of wisdom for everyone to consider that he is but a man, and therefore he should not pitch his soaring thoughts beyond the level of mortality, but imp the wings of his towering ambition, and obligingly submit and condescend to the weakness of others, it being many times a piece of complaisance to go out of the road for company's sake. No (say you), this is a grand piece of Folly: true, but yet all our living is no more than such kind of fooling: which though it may seem harsh to assert, yet it is not so strange as true.

For the better making it out it might perhaps be requisite to invoke the aid of the muses, to whom the poets devoutly apply themselves upon far more slender occasions. Come then and assist, ye Heliconian lasses, while I attempt to prove that there is no method for an arrival at wisdom, and consequently no track to the goal of happiness, without the instructions and directions of Folly.

And here, in the first place it has been already acknowledged, that all the passions are listed under my regiment, since this is resolved to be the only distinction betwixt a wise man and a fool, that this latter is governed by passion, the other guided by reason: and therefore the Stoics look upon passions no other than as the infection and malady of the soul that disorders the constitution of the whole man, and by putting the spirits into a feverish ferment many times occasion some mortal distemper. And yet these, however decried, are not only our tutors to instruct us towards the attainment of wisdom, but even bolden us likewise, and spur us on to a quicker dispatch of all our undertakings. This, I suppose, will be stomached by the stoical Seneca, who pretends that the only emblem of wisdom is the man without passion; whereas the supposing any person to be so, is perfectly to unman him, or else transforming him into some fabulous deity that never was, nor ever will be; nay, to speak more plain, it is but the making him a mere statue, immoveable, senseless, and altogether inactive. And if this be their wise man, let them take him to themselves, and remove him into Plato's commonwealth, the new Atlantis, or some other-like fairy land. For who would not hate and avoid such a person as should be deaf to all the dictates of common sense? That should have no more power of love or pity than a block or stone, that remains heedless of all dangers? That thinks he can never mistake, but can foresee all contingencies at the greatest distance, and make provision for the worst presages? That feeds upon himself and his own thoughts, that monopolises health, wealth, power, dignity, and all to himself? That loves no man, nor is beloved of any? That has the

Fools have the Privilege of Speaking the Truth.

impudence to tax even divine providence of ill contrivance, and proudly grudges, nay, tramples under foot all other men's reputation; and this is he that is the Stoic's complete wise man. But prithee what city would choose such a magistrate? What army would be willing to serve under such a commander? Or what woman would be content with such a do-little husband? Who would invite such a guest? Or what servant would be retained by such a master? The most illiterate mechanic would in all respects be a more acceptable man, who would be frolicsome with his wife, free with his friends, jovial at a feast, pliable in converse, and obliging to all company. But I am tired out with this part of my subject, and so must pass to some other topics.

And now were anyone placed on that tower, from whence Jove is fancied by the poets to survey the world, he would all around discern how many grievances and calamities our whole life is on every side encom-passed with: how unclean our birth, how troublesome our tendance in the cradle, how liable our childhood is to a thousand misfortunes, how toil-some and full of drudgery our riper years, how heavy and uncomfortable our old age, and lastly, how unwelcome the unavoidableness of death. Farther, in every course of life how many wracks there may be of torturing diseases, how many unhappy accidents may casually occur, how many unex-pected disasters may arise, and what strange alterations may one moment produce? Not to mention such miseries as men are mutually the cause of, as poverty, imprisonment, slander, reproach, revenge, treachery, malice, cousenage, deceit, and so many more, as to reckon them all would be as puzzling arithmetic as the numbering of the sands.

How mankind became environed with such hard circumstances, or what deity imposed these plagues, as a penance on rebellious mortals, I am not now at leisure to enquire: but whoever seriously takes them into consideration must needs commend the valour of the Milesian virgins, who voluntarily killed themselves to get rid of a troublesome world; and how many wise men have taken the same course of becoming their own executioners; among whom, not to mention Diogenes, Xenocrates, Cato, Cassius, Brutus, and other heroes, the self-denying Chiron is never enough to be commended; who, when he was offered by Apollo the privi-lege of being exempted from death, and living on to the world's end, he refused the enticing proposal, as deservedly thinking it a punishment rather than a reward.

But if all were thus wise you see how soon the world would be unpeo-pled, and what need there would be of a second Prometheus, to plaister up

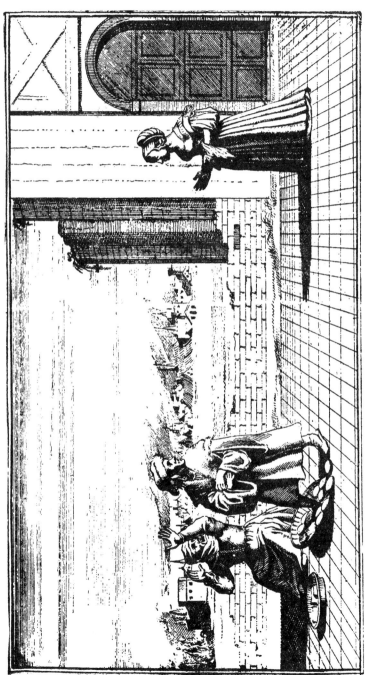

Folly among the Greeks and Latins.

the decayed image of mankind. I therefore come and stand in this gap of danger, and prevent farther mischief; partly by ignorance, partly by inadvertence; by the oblivion of whatever would be grating to remember, and the hopes of whatever may be grateful to expect, together palliating all griefs with an intermixture of pleasure; whereby I make men so far from being weary of their lives, that when their thread is spun to its full length, they are yet unwilling to die, and mighty hardly brought to take their last farewell of their friends. Thus some decrepit old fellows, that look as hollow as the grave into which they are falling, that rattle in the throat at every word they speak, that can eat no meat but what is tender enough to suck, that have more hair on their beard than they have on their head, and go stooping toward the dust they must shortly return to; whose skin seems already drest into parchment, and their bones already dried to a skeleton; these shadows of men shall be wonderful ambitious of living longer, and therefore fence off the attacks of death with all imaginable sleights and impostures; one shall new dye his grey hairs, for fear their colour should betray his age; another shall spruce himself up in a light periwig; a third shall repair the loss of his teeth with an ivory set; and a fourth perhaps shall fall deeply in love with a young girl, and accordingly court her with as much of gaiety and briskness as the liveliest spark in the whole town: and we cannot but know, that for an old man to marry a young wife without a portion, to be a cooler to other men's lust, is grown so common, that it is become the a-la-mode of the times. And what is yet more comical, you shall have some wrinkled old women, whose very looks are a sufficient antidote to lechery, that shall be canting out, *Ah, life is a sweet thing*, and so run a caterwauling, and hire some strong-backed stallions to recover their almost lost sense of feeling; and to set themselves off the better, they shall paint and daub their faces, always stand a tricking up themselves at their looking-glass, go naked-necked, bare-breasted, be tickled at a smutty jest, dance among the young girls, write love letters, and do all the other little knacks of decoying hot-blooded suitors; and in the meanwhile, however they are laughed at, they enjoy themselves to the full, live up to their hearts' desire, and want for nothing that may complete their happiness. As for those that think them herein so ridiculous, I would have them give an ingenuous answer to this one query, whether if folly or hanging were left to their choice, they had not much rather live like fools, than die like dogs? But what matter is it if these things are resented by the vulgar? Their ill word is no injury to fools, who are either altogether insensible of any affront, or at least lay it not much to heart. If they were knocked on the

head, or had their brains dashed out, they would have some cause to complain; but alas, slander, calumny, and disgrace, are no other way injurious
than as they are interpreted; nor otherwise evil, than as they are thought
to be so: what harm is it then if all persons deride and scoff you, if you bear
but up in your own thoughts, and be yourself thoroughly conceited of
your deserts? And prithee, why should it be thought any scandal to be a
fool, since the being so is one part of our nature and essence; and as so,
our not being wise can no more reasonably be imputed as a fault, than it
would be proper to laugh at a man because he cannot fly in the air like
birds and fowls; because he goes not on all four as beasts of the field;
because he does not wear a pair of visible horns as a crest on his forehead,
like bulls or stags: by the same figure we may call a horse unhappy, because
he was never taught his grammar; and an ox miserable, for that he never
learnt to fence: but sure as a horse for not knowing a letter is nevertheless
valuable, so a man, for being a fool, is never the more unfortunate, it
being by nature and providence so ordained for each.

Ay, but (say our patrons of wisdom) the knowledge of arts and sciences
is purposely attainable by men, that the defect of natural parts may be sup-
plied by the help of acquired: as if it were probable that nature, which had
been so exact and curious in the mechanism of flowers, herbs, and flies,
should have bungled most in her masterpiece, and made man as it were
by halves, to be afterward polished and refined by his own industry, in the
attainment of such sciences as the Egyptians feigned were invented by
their god Theuth, as a sure plague and punishment to mankind, being so
far from augmenting their happiness, that they do not answer that end
they were first designed for, which was the improvement of memory, as
Plato in his Phædrus does wittily observe.

In the first golden age of the world there was no need of these
perplexities; there was then no other sort of learning but what was
naturally collected from every man's common sense, improved by an easy
experience. What use could there have been of grammar, when all men
spoke the same mother-tongue, and aimed at no higher pitch of oratory,
than barely to be understood by each other? What need of logic, when they
were too wise to enter into any dispute? Or what occasion for rhetoric,
where no difference arose to require any laborious decision? And as little
reason had they to be tied up by any laws, since the dictates of nature
and common morality were restraint and obligation sufficient: and as to
all the mysteries of providence, they made them rather the object of their

The Begging Friar.

The First Scene of Infancy.

wonder, than their curiosity; and therefore were not so presumptuous as to dive into the depths of nature, to labour for the solving all phenomena in astronomy, or to wrack their brains in the splitting of entities, and unfolding the nicest speculations, judging it a crime for any man to aim at what is put beyond the reach of his shallow apprehension.

Thus was ignorance, in the infancy of the world, as much the parent of happiness as it has been since of devotion: but as soon as the golden age began by degrees to degenerate into more drossy metals, then were arts likewise invented; yet at first but few in number, and those rarely understood, till in farther process of time the superstition of the Chaldeans, and the curiosity of the Grecians, spawned so many subtleties, that now it is scarce the work of an age to be thoroughly acquainted with all the criticisms in grammar only. And among all the several Arts, those are proportionably most esteemed that come nearest to weakness and folly. For thus divines may bite their nails, and naturalists may blow their fingers, astrologers may know their own fortune is to be poor, and the logician may shut his fist and grasp the wind.

> While all these hard-named fellows cannot make
> So great a figure as a single quack.

And in this profession, those that have most confidence, though the least skill, shall be sure of the greatest custom; and indeed this whole art as it is now practised, is but one incorporated compound of craft and imposture.

Next to the physician comes (he, who perhaps will commence a suit with me for not being placed before him, I mean) the lawyer, who is so silly as to be *ignoramus* to a proverb, and yet by such are all difficulties resolved, all controversies determined, and all affairs managed so much to their own advantage, that they get those estates to themselves which they are employed to recover for their clients: while the poor divine in the mean time shall have the lice crawl upon his threadbare gown, before, by all his sweat and drudgery, he can get money enough to purchase a new one. As those arts therefore are most advantageous to their respective professors which are farthest distant from wisdom, so are those persons incomparably most happy that have least to do with any at all, but jog on in the common road of nature, which will never mislead us, except we voluntarily leap over those boundaries which she has cautiously set to our finite beings. Nature glitters most in her own plain, homely garb, and then gives the greatest lustre when she is unsullied from all artificial garnish.

Thus if we enquire into the state of all dumb creatures, we shall find those fare best that are left to nature's conduct: as to instance in bees, what is more to be admired than the industry and contrivance of these little animals? What architect could ever form so curious a structure as they give a model of in their inimitable combs? What kingdom can be governed with better discipline than they exactly observe in their respective hives? While the horse, by turning a rebel to nature, and becoming a slave to man, undergoes the worst of tyranny: he is sometimes spurred on to battle so long till he draw his guts after him for trapping, and at last falls down, and bites the ground instead of grass; not to mention the penalty of his jaws being curbed, his tail docked, his back wrung, his sides spur-galled, his close imprisonment in a stable, his rapshin and fetters when he runs a grass, and a great many other plagues, which he might have avoided, if he had kept to that first station of free-dom which nature placed him in. How much more desirable is the unconfined range of flies and birds, who living by instinct, would want nothing to complete their happiness, if some well-employed Domitian would not persecute the former, nor the sly fowler lay snares and gins for the entrapping of the other? And if young birds, before their unfledged wings can carry them from their nests, are caught, and pent up in a cage, for the being taught to sing, or whistle, all their new tunes make not half so sweet music as their wild notes, and natural melody: so much does that which is but rough-drawn by nature surpass and excel all the additional paint and varnish of art. And we cannot sure but commend and admire that Pythagorean cock, which (as Lucian relates) had been successively a man, a woman, a prince, a subject, a fish, a horse, and a frog; after all his experience, he summed up his judgment in this censure, that man was the most wretched and deplorable of all creatures, all other patiently grazing within the enclosures of nature, while man only broke out, and strayed beyond those safer limits, which he was justly confined to. And Gryllus is to be adjudged wiser than the much-counselling Ulysses, in as much as when by the enchantment of Circe he had been turned into a hog, he would not lay down his swinishness, nor forsake his beloved sty, to run the peril of a hazardous voyage. For a farther confir-mation whereof I have the authority of Homer, that captain of all poetry, who, as he gives to mankind in general, the epithet of wretched and unhappy, so he bestows in particular upon Ulysses the title of miserable, which he never attributes to Paris, Ajax, Achilles, or any other of the

The Lawyer.

The Old Man Spruced Up.

commanders; and that for this reason, because Ulysses was more crafty, cautious, and wise, than any of the rest.

As those therefore fall shortest of happiness that reach highest at wisdom, meeting with the greater repulse for soaring beyond the boundaries of their nature, and without remembering themselves to be but men, like the fallen angels, daring them to vie with Omnipotence, and giant-like scale heaven with the engines of their own brain; so are those most exalted in the road of bliss that degenerate nearest into brutes, and quietly divest themselves of all use and exercise of reason.

And this we can prove by a familiar instance. As namely, can there be anyone sort of men that enjoy themselves better than those which we call idiots, changelings, fools and naturals? It may perhaps sound harsh, but upon due consideration it will be found abundantly true, that these persons in all circumstances fare best, and live most comfortably; as first, they are void of all fear, which is a very great privilege to be exempted from; they are troubled with no remorse, nor pricks of conscience; they are not frighted with any bugbear stories of another world; they startle not at the fancied appearance of ghosts, or apparitions; they are not wracked with the dread of impending mischiefs, nor bandied with the hopes of any expected enjoyments: in short, they are unassaulted by all those legions of cares that war against the quiet of rational souls; they are ashamed of nothing, fear no man, banish the uneasiness of ambition, envy, and love; and to add the reversion of a future happiness to the enjoyment of a present one, they have no sin neither to answer for; divines unanimously maintaining, that a gross and unavoidable ignorance does not only extenuate and abate from the aggravation, but wholly expiate the guilt of any immorality.

Come now then as many of you as challenge the respect of being accounted wise, ingenuously confess how many insurrections of rebellious thoughts, and pangs of a labouring mind, ye are perpetually thrown and tortured with; reckon up all those inconveniences that you are unavoidably subject to, and then tell me whether fools, by being exempted from all these embroilments, are not infinitely more free and happy than yourselves? Add to this, that fools do not barely laugh, and sing, and play the good-fellow alone to themselves: but as it is the nature of good to be communicative, so they impart their mirth to others, by making sport for the whole company they are at anytime engaged in, as if providence purposely designed them for an antidote to melancholy:

The Capuchin.

whereby they make all persons so fond of their society, that they are welcomed to all places, hugged, caressed, and defended, a liberty given them of saying or doing anything; so well beloved, that none dares to offer them the least injury; nay, the most ravenous beasts of prey will pass them by untouched, as if by instinct they were warned that such innocence ought to receive no hurt. Farther, their converse is so acceptable in the court of princes, that few kings will banquet, walk, or take any other diversion, without their attendance; nay, and had much rather have their company, than that of their gravest counsellors, whom they maintain more for fashion-sake than goodwill; nor is it so strange that these fools should be preferred before graver politicians, since these last, by their harsh, sour advice, and ill-timing the truth, are fit only to put a prince out of the humour, while the others laugh, and talk, and joke, without any danger of disobliging.

It is one farther very commendable property of fools, that they always speak the truth, than which there is nothing more noble and heroical. For so, though Plato relate it as a sentence of Alcibiades, that in the sea of drunkenness truth swims uppermost, and so wine is the only teller of truth, yet this character may more justly be assumed by me, as I can make good from the authority of Euripides, who lays down this as an axiom μωρὰ μωρός λέγει, Children and fools always speak the truth. Whatever the fool has in his heart he betrays it in his face; or what is more notifying, discovers it by his words: while the wise man, as Euripides observes, carries a double tongue; the one to speak what may be said, the other what ought to be; the one what truth, the other what the time requires: whereby he can in a trice so alter his judgment, as to prove that to be now white, which he had just before swore to be black; like the satyr at his porridge, blowing hot and cold at the same breath; in his lips professing one thing, when in his heart he means another.

Furthermore, princes in their greatest splendour seem upon this account unhappy, in that they miss the advantage of being told the truth, and are shammed off by a parcel of insinuating courtiers, that acquit themselves as flatterers more than as friends. But some will perchance object, that princes do not love to hear the truth and therefore wise men must be very cautious how they behave themselves before them, lest they should take too great a liberty in speaking what is true, rather than what is acceptable. This must be confessed, truth indeed is seldom palatable to the ears of kings; yet fools have so great a privilege as to have free leave, not only to speak bare truths, but the most bitter ones too; so as the same reproof, which had it come from the mouth of a wise man would have cost him his head, being blurted out by a fool, is not only pardoned, but well taken, and rewarded. For truth has naturally a mixture of pleasure, if it carry with it nothing of offence to the person whom it is applied to; and the happy knack of ordering it so is bestowed only on fools. 'Tis for the same reason that this sort of men are more fondly beloved by women, who like their tumbling them about, and playing with them, though never so boisterously; pretending to take that only in jest, which they would have to be meant in earnest, as that sex is very ingenious in palliating, and dissembling the bent of their wanton inclinations.

But to return. An additional happiness of these fools appears farther in this, that when they have run merrily on to their last stage of life, they neither find any fear nor feel any pain to die, but march contentedly to the other world, where their company sure must be as acceptable as it was here upon earth.

Let us draw now a comparison between the condition of a fool and that of a wise man, and see how infinitely the one outweighs the other.

Give me any instance then of a man as wise as you can fancy him possible to be, that has spent all his younger years in poring upon books, and trudging after learning, in the pursuit whereof he squanders away the pleasantest time of his life in watching, sweat, and fasting; and in his latter days he never tastes one mouthful of delight, but is always stingy, poor, dejected, melancholy, burthensome to himself, and unwelcome to others, pale, lean, thin-jawed, sickly, contracting by his sedentariness such hurtful distempers as bring him to an untimely death, like roses plucked before they shatter. Thus have you the draught of a wise man's happiness, more the object of a commiserating pity, than of an ambitioning envy.

But now again come the croaking Stoics, and tell me in mood and figure, that nothing is more miserable than the being mad: but the being a fool is the being mad, therefore there is nothing more miserable than the being a fool. Alas, this is but a fallacy, the discovery whereof solves the force of the whole syllogism. Well then, they argue subtlely, 'tis true; but as Socrates in Plato makes two Venuses and two Cupids, and shews how their actions and properties ought not to be confounded; so these disputants, if they had not been mad themselves, should have distinguished between a double madness in others: and there is certainly a great difference in the nature as well as in the degrees of them, and they are not both equally scandalous: for Horace seems to take delight in one sort, when he says:

The Commentator.

Does welcome frenzy make me thus mistake?

And Plato in his Phædon ranks the madness of poets, of prophets, and of lovers among those properties which conduce to a happy life. And Virgil, in the sixth Æneid, gives this epithet to his industrious Æneas:

If you will proceed to these your mad attempts.

And indeed there is a two-fold sort of madness; the one that which the furies bring from hell; those that are herewith possessed are hurried on to wars and contentions, by an inexhaustible thirst of power and riches, inflamed to some infamous and unlawful lust, enraged to act the parricide, seduced to become guilty of incest, sacrilege, or some other of those crimson-dyed crimes; or, finally, to be so pricked in conscience as to be lashed and stung with the whips and snakes of grief and remorse. But there is another sort of madness that proceeds from Folly, so far from being anyway injurious or distasteful that it is thoroughly good and desirable; and this happens when by a harmless mistake in the judgment of things the mind is freed from those cares which would otherwise gratingly afflict it, and smoothed over with a content and satisfaction it could not under other circumstances so happily enjoy. And this is that comfortable apathy or insensibleness which Cicero, in an epistle to his friend Atticus, wishes himself master of, that he might the less take to heart those insufferable outrages committed by the tyrannizing triumvirate, Lepidus, Antonius, and Augustus. That Grecian likewise had a happy time of it, who was so frantic as to sit a whole day in the empty theatre laughing, shouting, and clapping his hands, as if he had really seen some pathetic tragedy acted to the life, when indeed all was no more than the strength of imagination, and the efforts of delusion, while in all other respects the same person behaved himself very discreetly was,

Sweet to his friends, to his wife, obliging, kind,
And so averse from a revengeful mind,
That had his men unsealed his bottled wine,
He would not fret, nor doggedly repine.

And when by a course of physic he was recovered from this frenzy, he looked upon his cure so far from a kindness, that he thus reasons the case with his friends:

This remedy, my friends, is morse i' th' main
Than the disease, the cure augments the pain;
My only hope is a relapse again.

And certainly they were the more mad of the two who endeavoured to bereave him of so pleasing a delirium, and recall all the aches of his head by dispelling the mists of his brain. I have not yet determined whether it be proper to include all the defects of sense and understanding under the common genius of madness. For if anyone be so short-sighted as to take a mule for an ass, or so shallowpated as to admire a paltry ballad for an elegant poem, he is not thereupon immediately censured as mad. But if anyone let not only his senses but his judgment be imposed upon in the most ordinary common concerns, he shall come under the scandal of being thought next door to a madman. As suppose anyone should hear an ass bray, and should take it for ravishing music; or if anyone, born a beggar, should fancy himself as great as a prince, or the like. But this sort of madness, if (as is most usual) it be accompanied with pleasure, brings a great satisfaction both to those who are possessed with it themselves, and those who deride it in others, though they are not both equally frantic. And this species of madness is of larger extent than the world commonly imagines. Thus the whole tribe of madmen make sport among themselves, while one laughs at another; he that is more mad many times jeering him that is less so. But indeed the greater each man's madness is, the greater is his happiness, if it be but such a sort as proceeds from an excess of folly, which is so epidemical a distemper that it is hard to find anyone man so uninfected as not to have sometimes a fit or two of some sort of frenzy. There is only this difference between the several patients, he that shall take a broomstick for a strait-bodied woman is without more ado sentenced for a madman, because this is so strange a blunder as very seldom happens; whereas he whose wife is a common jilt, that keeps a warehouse free for all customers, and yet swears she is as chaste as an untouched virgin, and hugs himself in his contented mistake, is scarce taken notice of, because he fares no worse than a great many more of his good-natured neighbours. Among these are to be ranked such as take an immoderate delight in hunting, and think no music comparable to the sounding of horns and the yelping of beagles; and were they to take physic, would no question think the most sovereign virtues to be in the *album Græcum* of a dog's turd. When they have

The Daily Tally of Psalms.

The Last shall be First, and the First, Last.

The Mystery of Fate.

run down their game, what strange pleasure they take in cutting of it up! Cows and sheep may be slaughtered by common butchers, but what is killed in hunting must be broke up by none under a gentleman, who shall throw down his hat, fall devoutly on his knees, and drawing out a slashing hanger (for a common knife is not good enough), after several ceremonies shall dissect all the parts as artificially as the best skilled anatomist, while all that stand round shall look very intently, and seem to be mightily surprised with the novelty, though they have seen the same an hundred times before; and he that can but dip his finger, and taste of the blood, shall think his own bettered by it: and though the constant feeding on such diet does but assimilate them to the nature of those beasts they eat of, yet they will swear that venison is meat for princes, and that their living upon it makes them as great as emperors.

Near a kin to these are such as take a great fancy for building: they raise up, pull down, begin anew, alter the model, and never rest till they run themselves out of their whole estate, taking up such a compass for buildings, till they leave themselves not one foot of land to live upon, nor one poor cottage to shelter themselves from cold and hunger: and yet all the while are mighty proud of their contrivances, and sing a sweet *requiem* to their own happiness.

To these are to be added those plodding virtuosos, that plunder the most inward recesses of nature for the pillage of a new invention, and rake over sea and land for the turning up some hitherto latent mystery; and are so continually tickled with the hopes of success, that they spare for no cost nor pains, but trudge on, and upon a defeat in one attempt, courageously tack about to another, and fall upon new experiments, never giving over till they have calcined their whole estate to ashes, and have not money enough left unmelted to purchase one crucible or limbeck. And yet after all, they are not so much discouraged, but that they dream fine things still, and animate others what they can to the like undertakings; nay, when their hopes come to the last gasp, after all their disappointments, they have yet one *salvo* for their credit, that:

In great exploits our bare attempts suffice.

And so inveigh against the shortness of their life, which allows them not time enough to bring their designs to maturity and perfection.

Whether dice-players may be so favourably dealt with as to be admitted among the rest is scarce yet resolved upon: but sure it is hugely vain and

The Lazy Wretch.

ridiculous, when we see some persons so devoutly addicted to this diversion, that at the first rattle of the box their heart shakes within them, and keeps consort with the motion of the dice: they are egg'd on so long with the hopes of always winning, till at last, in a literal sense, they have thrown away their whole estate, and made shipwreck of all they have, scarce escaping to shore with their own clothes to their backs; thinking it in the meanwhile a great piece of religion to be just in the payment of their stakes, and will cheat any creditor sooner than him who trusts them in play: and that poring old men, that cannot tell their cast without the help of spectacles, should be sweating at the same sport; nay, that such decrepit blades, as by the gout have lost the use of their fingers, should look over, and hire others to throw for them. This indeed is prodigiously extravagant; but the consequence of it ends so oft in downright madness, that it seems rather to belong to the furies than to folly.

The next to be placed among the regiment of fools are such as make a trade of telling or inquiring after incredible stories of miracles and prodigies: never doubting that a lie will choke them, they will muster up a thousand several strange relations of spirits, ghosts, apparitions, raising of the devil, and such like bugbears of superstition, which the farther they are from being probably true, the more greedily they are swallowed, and the more devoutly believed. And these absurdities do not only bring an empty pleasure, and cheap divertisement, but they are a good trade, and procure a comfortable income to such priests and friars as by this craft get their gain. To these again are nearly related such others as attribute strange virtues to the shrines and images of saints and martyrs, and so would make their credulous proselytes believe, that if they pay their devotion to St. Christopher in the morning, they shall be guarded and secured the day following from all dangers and misfortunes: if soldiers, when they first take arms, shall come and mumble over such a set prayer before the picture of St. Barbara, they shall return safe from all engagements: or if any pray to Erasmus on such particular holidays, with the ceremony of wax candles, and other fopperies, he shall in a short time be rewarded with a plentiful increase of wealth and riches. The Christians have now their gigantic St. George, as well as the pagans had their Hercules; they paint the saint on horseback, and drawing the horse in splendid trappings, very gloriously accoutred, they scarce refrain in a literal sense from worshipping the very beast.

What shall I say of such as cry up and maintain the cheat of pardons and indulgences? That by these compute the time of each soul's residence in purgatory, and assign them a longer or shorter continuance, according as they purchase more or fewer of these paltry pardons, and saleable exemptions? Or what can be said bad enough of others, who pretend that by the force of such magical charms, or by the fumbling over their beads in the rehearsal of such and such petitions (which some religious impostors invented, either for diversion, or what is more likely for advantage), they shall procure riches, honour, pleasure, health, long life, a lusty old age, nay, after death a sitting at the right hand of our Saviour in His kingdom; though as to this last part of their happiness, they care not how long it be deferred, having scarce any appetite toward a tasting the joys of heaven, till they are surfeited, glutted with, and can no longer relish their enjoyments on earth. By this easy way of purchasing pardons, any notorious highwayman, any plundering soldier, or any bribe-taking judge, shall disburse some part of their unjust gains, and so think all their grossest impieties sufficiently atoned for; so many perjuries, lusts, drunkenness, quarrels, bloodsheds, cheats, treacheries, and all sorts of debaucheries, shall all be, as it were, struck a bargain for, and such a contract made, as if they had paid off all arrears, and might now begin upon a new score.

And what can be more ridiculous, than for some others to be confident of going to heaven by repeating daily those seven verses out of the Psalms, which the devil taught St. Bernard, thinking thereby to have put a trick upon him, but that he was overreached in his cunning.

Several of these fooleries, which are so gross and absurd, as I myself am even ashamed to own, are practised and admired, not only by the vulgar, but by such proficients in religion as one might well expect should have more wit.

From the same principles of folly proceeds the custom of each country's challenging their particular guardian-saint; nay, each saint has his distinct office allotted to him, and is accordingly addressed to upon the respective occasions: as one for the toothache, a second to grant an easy delivery in childbirth, a third to help persons to lost goods, another to protect seamen in a long voyage, a fifth to guard the farmer's cows and sheep, and so on; for to rehearse all instances would be extremely tedious.

There are some more catholic saints petitioned to upon all occasions, as more especially the Virgin Mary, whose blind devotees think it manners now to place the mother before the Son.

And of all the prayers and intercessions that are made to these respective saints the substance of them is no more than downright Folly. Among all the trophies that for tokens of gratitude are hung upon the walls and

The Dice Players.

Profusely Lavish in Charity.

ceilings of churches, you shall find no relics presented as a memorandum of any that were ever cured of Folly, or had been made one dram the wiser.

One perhaps after shipwreck got safe to shore; another recovered when he had been run through by an enemy; one, when all his fellow-soldiers were killed upon the spot, as cunningly perhaps as cowardly, made his escape from the field; another, while he was a hanging, the rope broke, and so he saved his neck, and renewed his licence for practising his old trade of thieving; another broke gaol, and got loose; a patient, against his physician's will, recovered of a dangerous fever; another drank poison, which putting him into a violent looseness, did his body more good than hurt, to the great grief of his wife, who hoped upon this occasion to have become a joyful widow; another had his waggon overturned, and yet none of his horses lamed; another had caught a grievous fall, and yet recovered from the bruise; another had been tampering with his neighbour's wife, and escaped very narrowly from being caught by the enraged cuckold in the very act. After all these acknowledgments of escapes from such singular dangers, there is none (as I have before intimated) that return thanks for being freed from Folly; Folly being so sweet and luscious, that it is rather sued for as a happiness, than deprecated as a punishment. But why should I launch out into so wide a sea of superstitions?

Had I as many tongues as Argus eyes,
Briareus hands, they all would not suffice
Folly in all her shapes t'epitomize.

Almost all Christians being wretchedly enslaved to blindness and ignorance, which the priests are so far from preventing or removing, that they blacken the darkness, and promote the delusion; wisely foreseeing that the people (like cows, which never give down their milk so well as when they are gently stroked), would part with less if they knew more, their bounty proceeding only from a mistake of charity. Now if any grave wise man should stand up, and unseasonably speak the truth, telling everyone that a pious life is the only way of securing a happy death; that the best title to a pardon of our sins is purchased by a hearty abhorrence of our guilt, and sincere resolutions of amendment; that the best devotion which can be paid to any saints is to imitate them in their exemplary life: if he should proceed thus to inform them of their several mistakes, there would be quite another estimate put upon tears, watchings, masses, fastings, and other severities, which before were so much prized, as persons will now be vexed to lose that satisfaction they formerly found in them.

In the same predicament of fools are to be ranked such, as while they are yet living, and in good health, take so great a care how they shall be buried when they die, that they solemnly appoint how many torches, how many escutcheons, how many gloves to be given, and how many mourners they will have at their funeral; as if they thought they themselves in their coffins could be sensible of what respect was paid to their corpse; or as if they doubted they should rest a whit the less quiet in the grave if they were with less state and pomp interred.

Now though I am in so great haste, as I would not willingly be stopped or detained, yet I cannot pass by without bestowing some remarks upon another sort of fools; who, though their first descent was perhaps no better than from a tapster or tinker, yet highly value themselves upon their birth and parentage. One fetches his pedigree from Æneas, another from Brute, a third from king Arthur: they hang up their ancestors' worm-eaten pictures as records of antiquity, and keep a long list of their predecessors, with an account of all their offices and titles, while they themselves are but transcripts of their forefathers' dumb statues, and degenerate even into those very beasts which they carry in their coat of arms as ensigns of their nobility: and yet by a strong presumption of their birth and quality, they live not only the most pleasant and unconcerned themselves, but there are not wanting others too who cry up these brutes almost equal to the gods. But why should I dwell upon one or two instances of Folly, when there are so many of like nature. Conceitedness and self-love making many by strength of Fancy believe themselves happy, when otherwise they are really wretched and despicable. Thus the most ape-faced, ugliest fellow in the whole town, shall think himself a mirror of beauty: another shall be so proud of his parts, that if he can but mark out a triangle with a pair of compasses, he thinks he has mastered all the difficulties of geometry, and could outdo Euclid himself. A third shall admire himself for a ravishing musician, though he have no more skill in the handling of any instrument than a pig playing on the organs: and another that rattles in the throat as hoarse as a cock crows, shall be proud of his voice, and think he sings like a nightingale.

There is another very pleasant sort of madness, whereby persons assume to themselves whatever of accomplishment they discern in others. Thus the happy rich churl in Seneca, who had so short a memory, as he could not tell the least story without a servant standing by to prompt him,

St. Bernard and the Devil.

The Actor.

and was at the same time so weak that he could scarce go upright, yet he thought he might adventure to accept a challenge to a duel, because he kept at home some lusty, sturdy fellows, whose strength he relied upon instead of his own.

It is almost needless to insist upon the several professors of arts and sciences, who are all so egregiously conceited, that they would sooner give up their title to an estate in lands, than part with the reversion of their wits: among these, more especially stage-players, musicians, orators, and poets, each of which, the more of duncery they have, and the more of pride, the greater is their ambition: and how notoriously soever dull they be, they meet with their admirers; nay, the more silly they are the higher they are extolled; Folly (as we have before intimated) never failing of respect and esteem. If therefore everyone, the more ignorant he is, the greater satisfaction he is to himself, and the more commended by others, to what purpose is it to sweat and toil in the pursuit of true learning, which shall cost so many gripes and pangs of the brain to acquire, and when obtained, shall only make the laborious student more uneasy to himself, and less acceptable to others?

As nature in her dispensation of conceitedness has dealt with private persons, so has she given a particular smatch of self-love to each country and nation. Upon this account it is that the English challenge the prerogative of having the most handsome women, of the being most accomplished in the skill of music, and of keeping the best tables: the Scotch brag of their gentility, and pretend the genius of their native soil inclines them to be good disputants: the French think themselves remarkable for complaisance and good breeding: the Sorbonists of Paris pretend before any others to have made the greatest proficiency in polemic divinity: the Italians value themselves for learning and eloquence; and, like the Grecians of old, account all the world barbarians in respect of themselves; to which piece of vanity the inhabitants of Rome are more especially addicted, pretending themselves to be owners of all those heroic virtues, which their city so many ages since was deservedly famous for. The Venetians stand upon their birth and pedigree. The Grecians pride themselves in having been the first inventors of most arts, and in their country being famed for the product of so many eminent philosophers. The Turks, and all the other refuse of Mahometism, pretend they profess the only true religion, and laugh at all Christians for superstitious, narrow-souled fools. The Jews to this day expect their Messias as devoutly as they believe in their first

The Grammarian.

prophet Moses. The Spaniards challenge the repute of being accounted good soldiers. And the Germans are noted for their tall, proper stature, and for their skill in magick. But not to mention anymore, I suppose you are already convinced how great an improvement and addition to the happiness of human life is occasioned by self-love: next step to which is flattery; for as self-love is nothing but the coaxing up of ourselves, so the same currying and humouring of others is termed flattery.

Flattery, it is true, is now looked upon as a scandalous name, but it is by such only as mind words more than things. They are prejudiced against it upon this account, because they suppose it justles out all truth and sincerity? Whereas indeed its property is quite contrary, as appears from the examples of several brute creatures. What is more fawning than a spaniel? And yet what is more faithful to his master? What is more fond and loving than a tame squirrel? And yet what is more sporting and inoffensive? This little frisking creature is kept up in a cage to play withal, while lions, tigers, leopards, and such other savage emblems of rapine and cruelty are shewn only for state and rarity, and otherwise yield no pleasure to their respective keepers.

There is indeed a pernicious destructive sort of flattery wherewith rookers and sharks work their several ends upon such as they can make a prey of, by decoying them into traps and snares beyond recovery: but that which is the effect of folly is of a much different nature; it proceeds from a softness of spirit, and a flexibleness of good humour, and comes far nearer to virtue than that other extreme of friendship, namely, a stiff, sour, dogged moroseness: it refreshes our minds when tired, enlivens them when melancholy, reinforces them when languishing, invigorates them when heavy, recovers them when sick, and pacifies them when rebellious: it puts us in a method how to procure friends, and how to keep them; it entices children to swallow the bitter rudiments of learning; it gives a new ferment to the almost stagnated souls of old men; it both reproves and instructs principles without offence under the mask of commendation: in short, it makes every man fond and indulgent of himself, which is indeed no small part of each man's happiness, and at the same time renders him obliging and complaisant in all company, where it is pleasant to see how the asses rub and scratch one another.

This again is a great accomplishment to an orator, a greater to a physician, and the only one to a poet: in fine, it is the best sweetener to all afflictions, and gives a true relish to the otherwise insipid enjoyments of our whole life. Ay, but (say you) to flatter is to deceive; and to deceive is very harsh and hurtful: no, rather just contrary; nothing is more welcome and bewitching than the being deceived. They are much to be blamed for an undistinguishing head, that make a judgment of things according to what they are in themselves, when their whole nature consists barely in the opinions that are had of them. For all sublunary matters are enveloped in such a cloud of obscurity, that the short-sightedness of human understanding, cannot pry through and arrive to any comprehensive knowledge of them: hence the sect of academic philosophers have modestly resolved, that all things being no more than probable, nothing can be known as certain; or if there could, yet would it but interrupt and abate from the pleasure of a more happy ignorance. Finally, our souls are so fashioned and moulded, that they are sooner captivated by appearances, than by real truths; of which, if anyone would demand an example, he may find a very familiar one in churches, where, if what is delivered from the pulpit be a grave, solid, rational discourse, all the congregation grow weary, and fall asleep, till their patience be released; whereas if the preacher (pardon the impropriety of the word, the prater I would have said) be zealous, in his thumps of the cushion, antic gestures, and spend his glass in the telling of pleasant stories, his beloved shall then stand up, tuck their hair behind their ears, and be very devoutly attentive. So among the saints, those are most resorted to who are most romantic and fabulous: as for instance, a poetic St. George, a St. Christopher, or a St. Barbara, shall be oftener prayed to than St. Peter, St. Paul, nay, perhaps than Christ himself; but this, it is possible, may more properly be referred to another place.

In the mean while observe what a cheap purchase of happiness is made by the strength of fancy. For whereas many things even of inconsiderable value, would cost a great deal of pains and perhaps pelf, to procure; opinion spares charges, and yet gives us them in as ample a manner by conceit, as if we possessed them in reality. Thus he who feeds on such a stinking dish of fish, as another must hold his nose at a yard's distance from, yet if he feed heartily, and relish them palateably, they are to him as good as if they were fresh caught: whereas on the other hand, if anyone be invited to never so dainty a joul of sturgeon, if it go against his stomach to eat any, he may sit a hungry, and bite his nails with greater appetite than his victuals. If a woman be never so ugly and nauseous, yet if her husband can but think her handsome, it is all one to him as if she really were so: if any man have never so ordinary and smutty a draught, yet if he admires the excellency of it, and can suppose it to have been drawn by some old Apelles, or modern Vandyke, he is as proud of it as if it had really been

The Restorative of Youth.

Youth.

The Two Asses.

done by one of their hands. I knew a friend of mine that presented his bride with several false and counterfeit stones, making her believe that they were right jewels, and cost him so many hundred thousand crowns; under his mistake the poor woman was as choice of pebbles, and painted glass, as if they had been so many natural rubies and diamonds, while the subtle husband saved a great deal in his pocket, and yet made his wife as well pleased as if he had been at ten hundred times the cost. What difference is there between them that in the darkest dungeon, can with a platonic brain survey the whole world in idea, and him that stands in the open air, and takes a less deluding prospect of the universe? If the beggar in Lucian, that dreamt he was a prince, had never waked, his imaginary kingdom had been as great as a real one. Between him therefore that truly is happy, and him that thinks himself so, there is no perceivable distinction; or if any, the fool has the better of it: first, because his happiness costs him less, standing him only in the price of a single thought; and then, secondly, because he has more fellow-companions and partakers of his good fortune: for no enjoyment is comfortable where the benefit is not imparted to others; nor is any one station of life desirable, where we can have no converse with persons of the same condition with ourselves: and yet this is the hard fate of wise men, who are grown so scarce, that like Phœnixes, they appear but one in an age. The Grecians, it is true, reckoned up seven within the narrow precincts of their own country; yet I believe, were they to cast up their accounts anew, they would not find a half, nay, not a third part, of one in far larger extent.

Farther, when among the several good properties of Bacchus this is looked upon as the chief, namely, that he drowns the cares and anxieties of the mind, though it be indeed but for a short while; for after a small nap, when our brains are a little settled, they all return to their former corrodings: how much greater is the more durable advantage which I bring? While by one uninterrupted fit of being drunk in conceit, I perpetually cajole the mind with riots, revels, and all the excess and energy of joy.

Add to this, that I am so communicative and bountiful, as to let no one particular person pass without some token of my favour; whereas other deities bestow their gifts sparingly to their elect only. Bacchus has not thought fit that every soil should bear the same juice-yielding grape: Venus has not given to all a like portion of beauty: Mercury endows but few with the knack of an accomplished eloquence: Hercules gives not to all the same measure of wealth and riches: Jupiter has ordained but a few to be

Imaginary Excellence.

born to a kingdom: Mars in battle gives a complete victory but to one party; nay, he often makes them both losers: Apollo does not answer the expectation of all that consult his oracles: Jove oft thunders: Phœbus sometimes shoots the plague, or some other infection, at the point of his darts: and Neptune swallows down more than he bears up: not to mention their Ve-Jupiters, their Plutos, their Ate goddess of loss, their evil geniuses, and such other monsters of divinity, as had more of the hangman than the god in them, and were worshipped only to deprecate that hurt which used to be inflicted by them: I say, not to mention these, I am that high and mighty goddess, whose liberality is of as large an extent as her omnipotence: I give to all that ask: I never appear sullen, nor out of humour, nor ever demand any atonement or satisfaction for the omission of any ceremonious punctilio in my worship: I do not storm or rage, if mortals, in their addresses to the other gods pass me by unregarded, without the acknowledgment of any respect or application: whereas all the other gods are so scrupulous and exact, that it often proves less dangerous manfully to despise them, than sneakingly to attempt the difficulty of pleasing them. Thus some men are of that captious, froward humour, that a man had better be wholly strangers to them, than never so intimate friends.

Well, but there are none (say you) build any altars, or dedicate any temple to Folly. I admire (as I have before intimated) that the world should be so wretchedly ungrateful. But I am so good natured as to pass by and pardon this seeming affront, though indeed the charge thereof, as unnecessary, may well be saved; for to what purpose should I demand the sacrifice of frankincense, cakes, goats, and swine, since all persons everywhere pay me that more acceptable service, which all divines agree to be more effectual and meritorious, namely, an imitation of my communicable attributes? I do not therefore any way envy Diana for having her altars bedewed with human blood: I think myself then most religiously adored, when my respective devotees (as is their usual custom) conform themselves to my practice, transcribe my pattern, and so live the copy of me their original. And truly this pious devotion is not so much in use among christians as is much to be wished it were: for how many zealous votaries are there that pay so profound respect to the Virgin Mary, as to place lighted tapers even at noon day upon her altars? And yet how few of them copy after her untouched chastity, her modesty, and her other commendable virtues, in the imitation whereof consists the truest esteem of divine worship? Farther, why should I desire a temple, since the whole world is but one ample continued choir, entirely dedicated to my use and service? Nor do

I want worshippers at any place where the earth wants not inhabitants. And as to the manner of my worship, I am not yet so irrecoverably foolish, as to be prayed to by proxy, and to have my honour intermediately bestowed upon senseless images and pictures, which quite subvert the true end of religion; while the unwary supplicants seldom distinguish betwixt the things themselves and the objects they represent. The same respect in the meanwhile is paid to me in a more legitimate manner; for to me there are as many statues erected as there are moving fabrics of mortality; every person, even against his own will, carrying the image of me, i.e., the signal of Folly instamped on his countenance. I have not therefore the least tempting inducement to envy the more seeming state and splendour of the other gods, who are worshipped at set times and places; as Phœbus at Rhodes, Venus in her Cyprian isle, Juno in the city Argos, Minerva at Athens, Jupiter on the hill Olympus, Neptune at Tarentum, and Priapus in the town of Lampsacum; while my worship extending as far as my influence, the whole world is my one altar, whereon the most valuable incense and sacrifice is perpetually offered up.

But lest I should seem to speak this with more of confidence than truth, let us take a nearer view of the mode of men's lives, whereby it will be rendered more apparently evident what largesses I everywhere bestow, and how much I am respected and esteemed of persons, from the highest to the basest quality. For the proof whereof, it being too tedious to insist upon each particular, I shall only mention such in general as are most worthy the remark, from which by analogy we may easily judge of the remainder. And indeed to what purpose would it be singly to recount the commonalty and rabble of mankind, who beyond all question are entirely on my side? And for a token of their vassalage do wear my livery in so many older shapes, and more newly invented modes of Folly, that the lungs of a thousand Democrituses would never hold out to such a laughter as this subject would excite; and to these thousand must be superadded one more, to laugh at them as much as they do at the other.

It is indeed almost incredible to relate what mirth, what sport, what diversion, the grovelling inhabitants here on earth give to the above-seated gods in heaven: for these exalted deities spend their fasting sober hours in listening to those petitions that are offered up, and in succouring such as they are appealed to by for redress; but when they are a little entered at a glass of nectar, they then throw off all serious concerns, and go and place themselves on the ascent of some promontory in heaven, and from thence survey the little molehill of earth. And trust me, there cannot be a more

The Juice Yielding Grape.

The Worship of Descent.

An Apostle.

delightsome prospect, than to view such a theatre so stuffed and crammed with swarms of fools. One falls desperately in love, and the more he is slighted the more does his spaniel-like passion increase; another is wedded to wealth rather than to a wife; a third pimps for his own spouse, and is content to be a cuckold so he may wear his horns gilt; a fourth is haunted with a jealousy of his visiting neighbours; another sobs and roars, and plays the child, for the death of a friend or relation; and lest his own tears should not rise high enough to express the torrent of his grief, he hires other mourners to accompany the corpse to the grave, and sing its requiem in sighs and lamentations; another hypocritically weeps at the funeral of one whose death at heart he rejoices for; here a gluttonous cormorant, whatever he can scrape up, thrusts all into his guts to pacify the cryings of a hungry stomach; there a lazy wretch sits yawning and stretching, and thinks nothing so desirable as sleep and idleness; some are extremely industrious in other men's business, and sottishly neglectful of their own; some think themselves rich because their credit is great, though they can never pay, till they break, and compound for their debts; one is so covetous that he lives poor to die rich; one for a little uncertain gain will venture to cross the roughest seas, and expose his life for the purchase of a livelihood; another will depend on the plunders of war, rather than on the honest gains of peace; some will close with and humour such warm old blades as have a good estate, and no children of their own to bestow it upon; others practice the same art of wheedling upon good old women, that have hoarded and coffered up more bags than they know how to dispose of; both of these sly flatteries make fine sport for the gods, when they are beat at their own weapons, and (as oft happens) are gulled by those very persons they intended to make a prey of. There is another sort of base scoundrels in gentility, such scraping merchants, who although, for the better vent of their commodities they lie, swear, cheat, and practice all the intrigues of dishonesty, yet think themselves no way inferior to persons of the highest quality, only because they have raked together a plentiful estate; and there are not wanting such insinuating hangers on, as shall caress and compliment them with the greatest respect, in hopes to go snacks in some of their dishonest gains; there are others so infected with the philosophical paradox of banishing property, and having all things in common, that they make no conscience of fastening on, and purloining whatever they can get, and converting it to their own use and possession; there are some who are rich only in wishes, and yet while they barely dream of vast mountains of wealth, they are as happy as if their imaginary fancies commenced real truths; some put on the best side outermost, and starve themselves at home to appear gay and splendid abroad; one with an open-handed freedom spends all he lays his fingers on; another with a logic-fisted gripingness catches at and grasps all he can come within the reach of; one apes it about in the streets to court popularity; another consults his ease, and sticks to the confinement of a chimney-corner; many others are tugging hard at law for a trifle, and drive on an endless suit, only to enrich a deferring judge, or a knavish advocate; one is for new-modelling a settled government; another is for some notable heroical attempt; and a third by all means must travel a pilgrim to Rome, Jerusalem, or some shrine of a saint elsewhere, though he have no other business than the paying of a formal impertinent visit, leaving his wife and children to fast, while he himself forsooth is gone to pray. In short, if (as Lucian fancies Menippus to have done heretofore) any man could now again look down from the orb of the moon, he would see thick swarms as it were of flies and gnats, that were quarrelling with each other, justling, fighting, fluttering, skipping, playing, just new produced, soon after decaying, and then immediately vanishing; and it can scarce be thought how many tumults and tragedies so inconsiderate a creature as man does give occasion to, and that in so short a space as the small span of life; subject to so many casualties, that the sword, pestilence, and other epidemic accidents, shall many times sweep away whole thousands at a brush.

But hold; I should but expose myself too far, and incur the guilt of being roundly laughed at, if I proceed to enumerate the several kinds of the folly of the vulgar. I shall confine therefore my following discourse only to such as challenge the repute of wisdom, and seemingly pass for men of the soundest intellectuals. Among whom the Grammarians present themselves in the front, a sort of men who would be the most miserable, the most slavish, and the most hateful of all persons, if I did not in some way alleviate the pressures and miseries of their profession by blessing them with a bewitching sort of madness: for they are not only liable to those five curses, which they so oft recite from the first five verses of Homer, but to five hundred more of a worse nature; as always damned to thirst and hunger, to be choked with dust in their unswept schools (schools, shall I term them, or rather elaboratories, nay, bridewells, and houses of correction?), to wear out themselves in fret and drudgery; to be deafened with the noise of gaping boys; and in short, to be stifled with heat and stench; and yet they cheerfully dispense with all these inconveniences, and, by the help of a fond conceit, think themselves as happy as

The Pilgrim.

The Professor.

The Fabulous Story.

any men living: taking a great pride and delight in frowning and looking big upon the trembling urchins, in boxing, slashing, striking with the ferula, and in the exercise of all their other methods of tyranny; while thus lording it over a parcel of young, weak chits, they imitate the Cuman ass, and think themselves as stately as a lion, that domineers over all the inferior herd. Elevated with this conceit, they can hold filth and nastiness to be an ornament; can reconcile their nose to the most intolerable smells; and finally, think their wretched slavery the most arbitrary kingdom, which they would not exchange for the jurisdiction of the most sovereign potentate: and they are yet more happy by a strong persuasion of their own parts and abilities; for thus when their employment is only to rehearse silly stories, and poetical fictions, they will yet think themselves wiser than the best experienced philosopher; nay, they have an art of making ordinary people, such as their schoolboys' fond parents, to think them as considerable as their own pride has made them. Add hereunto this other sort of ravishing pleasure: when any of them has found out who was the mother of Anchises, or has lighted upon some old unusual word, such as *bubsequa, bovinator, manticulator,* or other like obsolete cramp terms; or can, after a great deal of poring, spell out the inscription of some battered monument; Lord! What joy, what triumph, what congratulating their success, as if they had conquered Africa, or taken Babylon the Great! When they recite some of their frothy, bombast verses, if any happen to admire them, they are presently flushed with the least hint of commendation, and devoutly thank Pythagoras for his grateful hypothesis, whereby they are now become actuated with a descent of Virgil's poetic soul. Nor is any divertisement more pleasant, than when they meet to flatter and curry one another; yet they are so critical, that if anyone hap to be guilty of the least slip, or seeming blunder, another shall presently correct him for it, and then to it they go in a tongue-combat, with all the fervour, spleen, and eagerness imaginable. May Priscian himself be my enemy if what I am now going to say be not exactly true. I knew an old Sophister that was a Grecian, a latinist, a mathematician, a philosopher, a musician, and all to the utmost perfection, who, after threescore years' experience in the world, had spent the last twenty of them only in drudging to conquer the criticisms of grammar, and made it the chief part of his prayers, that his life might be so long spared till he had learned how rightly to distinguish betwixt the eight parts of speech, which no grammarian, whether Greek or Latin, had yet accurately done. If any chance to have placed that as a conjunction which

The Rhetorician.

ought to have been used as an adverb, it is a sufficient alarm to raise a war for doing justice to the injured word. And since there have been as many several grammars, as particular grammarians (nay, more, for Aldus alone wrote five distinct grammars for his own share), the schoolmaster must be obliged to consult them all, sparing for no time nor trouble, though never so great, lest he should be otherwise posed in an unobserved criticism, and so by an irreparable disgrace lose the reward of all his toil. It is indifferent to me whether you call this folly or madness, since you must needs confess that it is by my influence these school-tyrants, though in never so despicable a condition, are so happy in their own thoughts, that they would not change fortunes with the most illustrious Sophi of Persia.

The Poets, however somewhat less beholden to me, own a professed dependence on me, being a sort of lawless blades, that by prescription claim a license to a proverb, while the whole intent of their profession is only to smooth up and tickle the ears of fools, that by mere toys and fabulous shams, with which (however ridiculous) they are so bolstered up in an airy imagination, as to promise themselves an everlasting name, and promise, by their balderdash, at the same time to celebrate the never-dying memory of others. To these rapturous wits self-love and flattery are never-failing attendants; nor do any prove more zealous or constant devotees to folly.

The Rhetoricians likewise, though they are ambitious of being ranked among the Philosophers, yet are apparently of my faction, as appears among other arguments, by this more especially; in that among their several topics of completing the art of oratory, they all particularly insist upon the knack of jesting, which is one species of folly; as is evident from the books of oratory wrote to Herennius, put among Cicero's work, but done by some other unknown author; and in Quintilian, that great master of eloquence, there is one large chapter spent in prescribing the methods of raising laughter: in short, they may well attribute a great efficacy to folly, since on any argument they can many times by a slight laugh over what they could never seriously confute.

Of the same gang are those scribbling fops, who think to eternize their memory by setting up for authors: among which, though they are all some way indebted to me, yet are those more especially so, who spoil paper in blotting it with mere trifles and impertinences. For as to those graver drudgers to the press, that write learnedly, beyond the reach of an ordinary reader, who durst submit their labours to the review of the most severe critic, these are not so liable to be envied for their honour, as to be pitied for their sweat and slavery. They make additions, alterations, blot out, write anew, amend, interline, turn it upside down, and yet can never please their fickle judgment, but that they shall dislike the next hour what they penned the former; and all this to purchase the airy commendations of a few understanding readers, which at most is but a poor reward for all their fastings, watchings, confinements, and brain-breaking tortures of invention. Add to this the impairing of their health, the weakening of their constitution, their contracting sore eyes, or perhaps turning stark blind; their poverty, their envy, their debarment from all pleasures, their hastening on old age, their untimely death, and what other inconveniences of a like or worse nature can be thought upon: and yet the recompense for all this severe penance is at best no more than a mouthful or two of frothy praise. These, as they are more laborious, so are they less happy than those other hackney scribblers which I first mentioned, who never stand much to consider, but write what comes next at a venture, knowing that the more silly their composures are, the more they will be bought up by the greater number of readers, who are fools and blockheads: and if they hap to be condemned by some few judicious persons, it is an easy matter by clamour to drown their censure, and to silence them by urging the more numerous commendations of others. They are yet the wisest who transcribe whole discourses from others, and then reprint them as their own. By doing so they make a cheap and easy seizure to themselves of that reputation which cost the first author so much time and trouble to procure. If they are at any time pricked a little in conscience for fear of discovery, they feed themselves however with this hope, that if they be at last found plagiaries, yet at least for sometime they have the credit of passing for the genuine authors. It is pleasant to see how all these several writers are puffed up with the least blast of applause, especially if they come to the honour of being pointed at as they walk along the streets, when their several pieces are laid open upon every bookseller's stall, when their names are embossed in a different character upon the title-page, sometime only with the two first letters, and sometime with fictious cramp terms, which few shall understand the meaning of; and of those that do, all shall not agree in their verdict of the performance; some censuring, others approving it, men's judgments being as different as their palates, that being toothsome to one which is unsavoury and nauseous to another: though it is a sneaking piece of cowardice for authors to put feigned names to their works, as if, like bastards of their brain, they were afraid to own them. Thus one styles himself Telemachus, another

The Divine.

Stelenus, a third Polycrates, another Thrasymachus, and so on. By the same liberty we may ransack the whole alphabet, and jumble together any letters that come next to hand. It is farther very pleasant when these coxcombs employ their pens in writing congratulatory epistles, poems, and panegyricks, upon each other, wherein one shall be complimented with the title of Alcæus, another shall be charactered for the incomparable Callimachus; this shall be commended for a completer orator than Tully himself; a fourth shall be told by his fellow-fool that the divine Plato comes short of him for a philosophic soul. Sometime again they take up the cudgels, and challenge out an antagonist, and so get a name by a combat at dispute and controversy, while the unwary readers draw sides according to their different judgments: the longer the quarrel holds the more irreconcilable it grows; and when both parties are weary, they each pretend themselves the conquerors, and both lay claim to the credit of coming off with victory. These fooleries make sport for wise men, as being highly absurd, ridiculous and extravagant. True, but yet these paper-combatants, by my assistance, are so flushed with a conceit of their own greatness, that they prefer the solving of a syllogism before the sacking of Carthage; and upon the defeat of a poor objection carry themselves more triumphant than the most victorious Scipio.

Nay, even the learned and more judicious, that have wit enough to laugh at the other's folly, are very much beholden to my goodness; which (except ingratitude have drowned their ingenuity), they must be ready upon all occasions to confess. Among these I suppose the lawyers will shuffle in for precedence, and they of all men have the greatest conceit of their own abilities. They will argue as confidently as if they spoke gospel instead of law; they will cite you six hundred several precedents, though not one of them come near to the case in hand; they will muster up the authority of judgments, deeds, glosses, and reports, and tumble over so many musty records, that they make their employ, though in itself easy, the greatest slavery imaginable; always accounting that the best plea which they have took most pains for.

To these, as bearing great resemblance to them, may be added logicians and sophisters, fellows that talk as much by rote as a parrot; who shall run down a whole gossiping of old women, nay, silence the very noise of a belfry, with louder clappers than those of the steeple; and if their unappeasable clamorousness were their only fault it would admit of some excuse; but they are at the same time so fierce and quarrelsome, that they will wrangle bloodily for the least trifle, and be so over intent and eager, that they many times lose their game in the chase and fright away that truth they are hunting for. Yet self-conceit makes these nimble disputants such doughty champions, that armed with three or four close-linked syllogisms, they shall enter the lists with the greatest masters of reason, and not question the foiling of them in an irresistible baffle: nay, their obstinacy makes them so confident of their being in the right, that all the arguments in the world shall never convince them to the contrary.

Next to these come the philosophers in their long beards and short cloaks, who esteem themselves the only favourites of wisdom, and look upon the rest of mankind as the dirt and rubbish of the creation: yet these men's happiness is only a frantic craziness of brain; they build castles in the air, and infinite worlds in a vacuum. They will give you to a hair's breadth the dimensions of the sun, moon, and stars, as easily as they would do that of a flaggon or pipkin: they will give a punctual account of the rise of thunder, of the origin of winds, of the nature of eclipses, and of all the other abstrusest difficulties in physics, without the least demur or hesitation, as if they had been admitted into the cabinet council of nature, or had been eyewitnesses to all the accurate methods of creation; though alas nature does but laugh at all their puny conjectures; for they never yet made one considerable discovery, as appears in that they are unanimously agreed in no one point of the smallest moment; nothing so plain or evident but what by some or other is opposed and contradicted. But though they are ignorant of the artificial contexture of the least insect, they vaunt however, and brag that they know all things, when indeed they are unable to construe the mechanism of their own body; nay, when they are so purblind as not to be able to see a stone's cast before them, yet they shall be as sharp-sighted as possible in spying-out ideas, universals, separate forms, first matters, quiddities, formalities, and a hundred such like niceties, so diminutively small, that were not their eyes extremely magnifying, all the art of optics could never make them discernible. But they then most despise the low grovelling vulgar when they bring out their parallels, triangles, circles, and other mathematical figures, drawn up in battalia, like so many spells and charms of conjuration in muster, with letters to refer to the explication of the several problems; hereby raising devils as it were, only to have the credit of laying them, and amusing the ordinary spectators into wonder, because they have not wit enough to understand the juggle. Of these some undertake to profess themselves judicial astrologers, pretending to keep correspondence with the stars, and so from their information can resolve any query; and though it is all

The Sophist.

but a presumptuous imposture, yet some to be sure will be so great fools as to believe them.

The divines present themselves next; but it may perhaps be most safe to pass them by, and not to touch upon so harsh a string as this subject would afford. Beside, the undertaking may be very hazardous; for they are a sort of men generally very hot and passionate; and should I provoke them, I doubt not would set upon me with a full cry, and force me with shame to recant, which if I stubbornly refuse to do, they will presently brand me for a heretic, and thunder out an excommunication, which is their spiritual weapon to wound such as lift up a hand against them. It is true, no men own a less dependence on me, yet have they reason to confess themselves indebted for no small obligations. For it is by one of my properties, self-love, that they fancy themselves, with their elder brother Paul, caught up into the third heaven, from whence, like shepherds indeed, they look down upon their flock, the laity, grazing as it were, in the vales of the world below. They fence themselves in with so many surrounders of magisterial definitions, conclusions, corollaries, propositions explicit and implicit, that there is no falling in with them; or if they do chance to be urged to a seeming nonplus, yet they find out so many evasions, that all the art of man can never bind them so fast, but that an easy distinction shall give them a starting-hole to escape the scandal of being baffled. They will cut asunder the toughest argument with as much ease as Alexander did the gordian knot; they will thunder out so many rattling terms as shall fright an adversary into conviction. They are exquisitely dexterous in unfolding the most intricate mysteries; they will tell you to a tittle all the successive proceedings of Omnipotence in the creation of the universe; they will explain the precise manner of original sin being derived from our first parents; they will satisfy you in what manner, by what degrees, and in how long a time, our Saviour was conceived in the Virgin's womb, and demonstrate in the consecrated wafer how accidents may subsist without a subject. Nay, these are accounted trivial, easy questions; they have yet far greater difficulties behind, which notwithstanding they solve with as much expedition as the former; as namely, whether supernatural generation requires any instant of time for its acting? Whether Christ, as a son, bears a double specifically distinct relation to God the Father, and his virgin mother? Whether this proposition is possible to be true, the first person of the Trinity hated the second? Whether God, who took our nature upon him in the form of a man, could as well have become a woman, a devil, a beast, a herb, or a stone? And were it so possible

The Schoolman.

that the Godhead had appeared in any shape of an inanimate substance, how he should then have preached his gospel? Or how have been nailed to the cross? Whether if St. Peter had celebrated the eucharist at the same time our Saviour was hanging on the cross, the consecrated bread would have been transubstantiated into the same body that remained on the tree? Whether in Christ's corporal presence in the sacramental wafer, his humanity be not abstracted from his Godhead? Whether after the resurrection we shall carnally eat and drink as we do in this life? There are a thousand other more sublimated and refined niceties of notions, relations, quantities, formalities, quiddities, hæccities, and such like abstrusities, as one would think no one could pry into, except he had not only such cat's eyes as to see best in the dark, but even such a piercing faculty as to see through an inch-board, and spy out what really never had any being. Add to these some of their tenets and opinions, which are so absurd and extravagant, that the wildest fancies of the Stoicks which they so much disdain and decry as paradoxes, seem in comparison just and rational; as their maintaining, that it is a less aggravating fault to kill a hundred men, than for a poor cobbler to set a stitch on the sabbath day; or, that it is more justifiable to do the greatest injury imaginable to others, than to tell the least lie ourselves. And these subtleties are alchymized to a more refined sublimate by the abstracting brains of their several schoolmen; the Realists, the Nominalists, the Thomists, the Albertists, the Occamists, the Scotists; these are not all, but the rehearsal of a few only, as a specimen of their divided sects; in each of which there is so much of deep learning, so much of unfathomable difficulty, that I believe the apostles themselves would stand in need of a new illuminating spirit, if they were to engage in any controversy with these new divines. St. Paul, no question, had a full measure of faith; yet when he lays down faith to be the substance of things not seen, these men carp at it for an imperfect definition, and would undertake to teach the apostles better logic. Thus the same holy author wanted for nothing of the grace of charity, yet (say they) he describes and defines it but very inaccurately, when he treats of it in the thirteenth chapter of his first epistle to the Corinthians. The primitive disciples were very frequent in administering the holy sacrament, breaking bread from house to house; yet should they be asked of the *Terminus a quo* and the *Terminus ad quem*, the nature of transubstantiation? The manner how one body can be in several places at the same time? The difference betwixt the several attributes of Christ in heaven, on the cross, and in the consecrated bread? What time is required for the transubstantiating the bread into flesh? How it can be done by a short sentence pronounced by the priest, which sentence is a species of discreet quantity, that has no permanent *punctum?* Were they asked (I say) these, and several other confused queries, I do not believe they could answer so readily as our mincing schoolmen now-a-days take a pride to do. They were well acquainted with the Virgin Mary, yet none of them undertook to prove that she was preserved immaculate from original sin, as some of our divines very hotly contend for. St. Peter had the keys given to him, and that by our Saviour himself, who had never entrusted him except he had known him capable of their manage and custody; and yet it is much to be questioned whether Peter was sensible of that subtlety broached by Scotus, that he may have the key of knowledge effectually for others, who has no knowledge actually in himself. Again, they baptized all nations, and yet never taught what was the formal, material, efficient, and final cause of baptism, and certainly never dreamt of distinguishing between a delible and an indelible character in this sacrament. They worshipped in the spirit, following their master's injunction, God is a spirit, and they which worship him, must worship him in spirit, and in truth; yet it does not appear that it was ever revealed to them how divine adoration should be paid at the same time to our blessed Saviour in heaven, and to his picture here below on a wall, drawn with two fingers held out, a bald crown, and a circle round his head. To reconcile these intricacies to an appearance of reason requires three-score years' experience in metaphysics.

Farther, the apostles often mention *Grace,* yet never distinguish between *gratia, gratis data,* and *gratia gratificans.* They earnestly exhort us likewise to good works, yet never explain the difference between *Opus operans,* and *Opus operatum.* They very frequently press and invite us to seek after charity, without dividing it into infused and acquired, or determining whether it be a substance or an accident, a created or an uncreated being. They detested sin themselves, and warned others from the commission of it; and yet I am sure they could never have defined so dogmatically, as the Scotists have since done. St. Paul, who in other's judgment is no less the chief of the apostles, than he was in his own the chief of sinners, who being bred at the feet of Gamaliel, was certainly more eminently a scholar than any of the rest, yet he often exclaims against vain philosophy, warns us from doting about questions and strifes of words, and charges us to avoid profane and vain babblings, and oppositions of science falsely so called; which he would not have done, if he had thought it worth his while to have become acquainted with them, which he might soon have

The Prayer for Forgiveness.

been, the disputes of that age being but small, and more intelligible sophisms, in reference to the vastly greater intricacies they are now improved to. But yet, however, our scholastic divines are so modest, that if they meet with any passage in St. Paul, or any other penman of holy writ, which is not so well modelled, or critically disposed of, as they could wish, they will not roughly condemn it, but bend it rather to a favorable interpretation, out of reverence to antiquity, and respect to the holy scriptures; though indeed it were unreasonable to expect anything of this nature from the apostles, whose lord and master had given unto them to know the mysteries of God, but not those of philosophy. If the same divines meet with anything of like nature unpalatable in St. Chrysostom, St. Basil, St. Hierom, or others of the fathers, they will not stick to appeal from their authority, and very fairly resolve that they lay under a mistake. Yet these ancient fathers were they who confuted both the Jews and Heathens, though they both obstinately adhered to their respective prejudices; they confuted them (I say), yet by their lives and miracles, rather than by words and syllogisms; and the persons they thus proselyted were downright honest, well meaning people, such as understood plain sense better than any artificial pomp of reasoning: whereas if our divines should now set about the gaining converts from paganism by their metaphysical subtleties, they would find that most of the persons they applied themselves to were either so ignorant as not at all to apprehend them, or so impudent as to scoff and deride them; or finally, so well skilled at the same weapons, that they would be able to keep their pass, and fence off all assaults of conviction: and this last way the victory would be altogether as hopeless, as if two persons were engaged of so equal strength, that it were impossible anyone should overpower the other.

If my judgment might be taken, I would advise Christians, in their next expedition to a holy war, instead of those many unsuccessful legions, which they have hitherto sent to encounter the Turks and Saracens, that they would furnish out their clamorous Scotists, their obstinate Occamists, their invincible Albertists, and all their forces of tough, crabbed and profound disputants: the engagement, I fancy, would be mighty pleasant, and the victory we may imagine on our side not to be questioned. For which of the enemies would not veil their turbans at so solemn an appearance? Which of the fiercest Janizaries would not throw away his scimitar, and all the half-moons be eclipsed by the interposition of so glorious an army?

I suppose you mistrust I speak all this by way of jeer and irony; and well I may, since among divines themselves there are some so ingenious as

Atlas Upholding the World.

to despise these captious and frivolous impertinences: they look upon it as a kind of profane sacrilege, and a little less than blasphemous impiety, to determine of such niceties in religion, as ought rather to be the subject of an humble and uncontradicting faith, than of a scrupulous and inquisitive reason: they abhor a defiling the mysteries of Christianity with an intermixture of heathenish philosophy, and judge it very improper to reduce divinity to an obscure speculative science, whose end is such a happiness as can be gained only by the means of practice. But alas, those notional divines, however condemned by the soberer judgment of others, are yet mightily pleased with themselves, and are so laboriously intent upon prosecuting their crabbed studies, that they cannot afford so much time as to read a single chapter in any one book of the whole bible. And while they thus trifle away their misspent hours in trash and babble, they think that they support the Catholic Church with the props and pillars of propositions and syllogisms, no less effectually than Atlas is feigned by the poets to sustain on his shoulders the burden of a tottering world. Their privileges, too, and authority are very considerable: they can deal with any text of scripture as with a nose of wax, knead it into what shape best suits their interest; and whatever conclusions they have dogmatically resolved upon, they would have them as irrepealably ratified as Solon's laws, and in as great force as the very decrees of the papal chair. If any be so bold as to remonstrate to their decisions, they will bring him on his knees to a recantation of his impudence. They shall pronounce as irrevocably as an oracle, this proposition is scandalous, that irreverent; this has a smack of heresy, and that is bald and improper; so that it is not the being baptised into the church, the believing of the scriptures, the giving credit to St. Peter, St. Paul, St. Hierom, St. Augustin, nay, or St. Thomas Aquinas himself, that shall make a man a Christian, except he have the joint suffrage of these novices in learning, who have blessed the world no doubt with a great many discoveries, which had never come to light, if they had not struck the fire of subtlety out of the flint of obscurity. These fooleries sure must be a happy employ.

Farther, they make as many partitions and divisions in hell and purgatory, and describe as many different sorts and degrees of punishment as if they were very well acquainted with the soil and situation of those infernal regions. And to prepare a seat for the blessed above, they invent new orbs, and a stately empyrean heaven, so wide and spacious as if they had purposely contrived it, that the glorified saints might have room enough to walk, to feast, or to take any recreation.

With these, and a thousand more such like toys, their heads are more stuffed and swelled than Jove, when he went big of Pallas in his brain, and was forced to use the midwifery of Vulcan's axe to ease him of his teeming burden. Do not wonder, therefore, that at public disputations they bind their heads with so many caps one over another; for this is to prevent the loss of their brains, which would otherwise break out from their uneasy confinement. It affords likewise a pleasant scene of laughter, to listen to these divines in their hotly managed disputations; to see how proud they are of talking such hard gibberish, and stammering out such blundering distinctions, as the auditors perhaps may sometimes gape at, but seldom apprehend: and they take such a liberty in their speaking of Latin, that they scorn to stick at the exactness of syntax or concord; pretending it is below the majesty of a divine to talk like a pedagogue, and be tied to the slavish observance of the rules of grammar. Finally, they take a vast pride, among other citations, to allege the authority of their respective master, which word they bear as profound a respect to as the Jews did to their ineffable *tetragrammaton*, and therefore they will be sure never to write it any otherwise than in great letters, MAGISTER NOSTER; and if any happen to invert the order of the words, and say, *noster magister*, instead of *magister noster*, they will presently exclaim against him as a pestilent heretic and underminer of the catholic faith.

The next to these are another sort of brainsick fools, who style them-selves monks and of religious orders, though they assume both titles very unjustly: for as to the last, they have very little religion in them; and as to the former, the etymology of the word monk implies a solitariness, or being alone; whereas they are so thick abroad that we cannot pass any street or alley without meeting them. Now I cannot imagine what one degree of men would be more hopelessly wretched, if I did not stand their friend, and buoy them up in that lake of misery, which by the engagements of a holy vow they have voluntarily immerged themselves in. But when these sort of men are so unwelcome to others, as that the very sight of them is thought ominous, I yet make them highly in love with themselves, and fond admirers of their own happiness. The first step whereunto they esteem a profound ignorance, thinking carnal knowledge a great enemy to their spiritual welfare, and seem confident of becoming greater proficients in divine mysteries the less they are poisoned with any human learning. They imagine that they bear a sweet consort with the heavenly choir, when they tone out their daily tally of psalms, which they rehearse only by rote, without permitting their understanding or affections to go along

Jove and Vulcan.

with their voice. Among these some make a good profitable trade of beggary, going about from house to house, not like the apostles, to break, but to beg, their bread; nay, thrust into all public-houses, come aboard the passage-boats, get into the travelling waggons, and omit no opportunity of time or place for the craving people's charity; doing a great deal of injury to common highway beggars by interloping in their traffic of alms. And when they are thus voluntarily poor, destitute, not provided with two coats, nor with any money in their purse, they have the impudence to pretend that they imitate the first disciples, whom their master expressly sent out in such an equipage. It is pretty to observe how they regulate all their actions as it were by weight and measure to so exact a proportion, as if the whole loss of their religion depended upon the omission of the least punctilio. Thus they must be very critical in the precise number of knots to the tying on of their sandals; what distinct colours their respective habits, and what stuff made of; how broad and long their girdles; how big, and in what fashion, their hoods; whether their bald crowns be to a hair's-breadth of the right cut; how many hours they must sleep, at what minute rise to prayers, &c. And these several customs are altered according to the humours of different persons and places. While they are sworn to the superstitious observance of these trifles, they do not only despise all others, but are very inclinable to fall out among themselves; for though they make profession of an apostolic charity, yet they will pick a quarrel, and be implacably passionate for such poor provocations, as the girting on a coat the wrong way, for the wearing of clothes a little too darkish coloured, or any such nicety not worth the speaking of. Some are so obstinately superstitious that they will wear their upper garment of some coarse dog's hair stuff, and that next their skin as soft as silk: but others on the contrary will have linen frocks outermost, and their shirts of wool, or hair. Some again will not touch a piece of money, though they make no scruple of the sin of drunkenness, and the lust of the flesh. All their several orders are mindful of nothing more than of their being distinguished from each other by their different customs and habits. They seem indeed not so careful of becoming like Christ, and of being known to be his disciples, as the being unlike to one another, and distinguishable for followers of their several founders. A great part of their religion consists in their title: some will be called cordeliers, and these subdivided into capuchines, minors, minims, and mendicants; some again are styled Benedictines, others of the order of St. Bernard, others of that of St. Bridget; some are Augustin monks, some Willielmites, and others Jacobists, as if the common name of

Christian were too mean and vulgar. Most of them place their greatest stress for salvation on a strict conformity to their foppish ceremonies, and a belief of their legendary traditions; wherein they fancy to have acquitted themselves with so much of supererogation, that one heaven can never be a condign reward for their meritorious life; little thinking that the Judge of all the earth at the last day shall put them off, with a who hath required these things at your hands; and call them to account only for the stewardship of his legacy, which was the precept of love and charity. It will be pretty to hear their pleas before the great tribunal: one will brag how he mortified his carnal appetite by feeding only upon fish: another will urge that he spent most of his time on earth in the divine exercise of singing psalms: a third will tell how many days he fasted, and what severe penance he imposed on himself for the bringing his body into subjection: another shall produce in his own behalf as many ceremonies as would load a fleet of merchantmen: a fifth shall plead that in threescore years he never so much as touched a piece of money, except he fingered it through a thick pair of gloves: a sixth, to testify his former humility, shall bring along with him his sacred hood, so old and nasty, that any seaman had rather stand bare headed on the deck, than put it on to defend his ears in the sharpest storms: the next that comes to answer for himself shall plead, that for fifty years together, he had lived like a sponge upon the same place, and was content never to change his homely habitation: another shall whisper softly, and tell the judge he has lost his voice by a continual singing of holy hymns and anthems: the next shall confess how he fell into a lethargy by a strict, reserved, and sedentary life: and the last shall intimate that he has forgot to speak, by having always kept silence, in obedience to the injunction of taking heed lest he should have offended with his tongue. But amidst all their fine excuses our Saviour shall interrupt them with this answer, Woe unto you, scribes and pharisees, hypocrites, verily I know you not; I left you but one precept, of loving one another, which I do not hear anyone plead he has faithfully discharged: I told you plainly in my gospel, without any parable, that my father's kingdom was prepared not for such as should lay claim to it by austerities, prayers, or fastings, but for those who should render themselves worthy of it by the exercise of faith, and the offices of charity: I cannot own such as depend on their own merits without a reliance on my mercy: as many of you therefore as trust to the broken reeds of your own deserts may even go search out a new heaven, for you shall never enter into that, which from the foundations of the world was prepared only for such as are true of heart. When these monks

John, the Baptist.

and friars shall meet with such a shameful repulse, and see that plough-men and mechanics are admitted into that kingdom, from which they themselves are shut out, how sneakingly will they look, and how pitifully slink away? Yet till this last trial they had more comfort of a future happi-ness, because more hopes of it than any other men. And these persons are not only great in their own eyes, but highly esteemed and respected by others, especially those of the order of mendicants, whom none dare to offer any affront to, because as confessors they are intrusted with all the secrets of particular intrigues, which they are bound by oath not to dis-cover; yet many times, when they are almost drunk, they cannot keep their tongue so far within their head, as not to be babbling out some hints, and shewing themselves so full, that they are in pain to be delivered. If any person give them the least provocation they will sure to be revenged of him, and in their next public harangue give him such shrewd wipes and reflections, that the whole congregation must needs take notice at whom they are levelled; nor will they ever desist from this way of declaiming, till their mouth be stopped with a bribe to hold their tongue. All their preach-ing is mere stage-playing, and their delivery the very transports of ridicule and drollery. Good Lord! How mimical are their gestures? What heights and falls in their voice? What toning, what bawling, what singing, what squeaking, what grimaces, making of mouths, apes' faces, and distorting of their countenance; and this art of oratory as a choice mystery, they con-vey down by tradition to one another. The manner of it I may adventure thus farther to enlarge upon. First, in a kind of mockery they implore the divine assistance, which they borrowed from the solemn custom of the poets: then if their text suppose be of charity, they shall take their exordi-um as far off as from a description of the river Nile in Egypt; or if they are to discourse of the mystery of the Cross, they shall begin with a story of Bell and the Dragon; or perchance if their subject be of fasting, for an entrance to their sermon they shall pass through the twelve signs of the zodiac; or lastly, if they are to preach of faith, they shall address themselves in a long mathematical account of the quadrature of the circle. I myself once heard a great fool (a great scholar I would have said) undertaking in a laborious discourse to explain the mystery of the Holy Trinity; in the unfolding whereof, that he might shew his wit and reading, and together satisfy itching ears, he proceeded in a new method, as by insisting on the letters, syllables, and proposition, on the concord of noun and verb, and that of noun substantive, and noun adjective; the auditors all wondered, and some mumbled to themselves that hemistitch of Horace,

Why all this needless trash?

But at last he brought it thus far, that he could demonstrate the whole Trinity to be represented by these first rudiments of grammar, as clearly and plainly as it was possible for a mathematician to draw a triangle in the sand: and for the making of this grand discovery, this subtle divine had plodded so hard for eight months together, that he studied himself as blind as a beetle, the intenseness of the eye of his understanding overshadowing and extinguishing that of his body; and yet he did not at all repent him of his blindness, but thinks the loss of his sight an easy purchase for the gain of glory and credit.

I heard at another time a grave divine, of fourscore years of age at least, so sour and hard-favoured, that one would be apt to mistrust that it was Scotus Redivivus; he taking upon him to treat of the mysterious name, JESUS, did very subtly pretend that in the very letters was contained, whatever could be said of it: for first, its being declined only with three cases, did expressly point out the trinity of persons, then that the nominative ended in S, the accusative in M, and the ablative in U, did imply some unspeakable mystery, viz., that in words of those initial letters Christ was the *summus*, or beginning, the *medius*, or middle, and the *ultimus*, or end of all things. There was yet a more abstruse riddle to be explained, which was by dividing the word "Jesus" into two parts, and separating the S in the middle from the two extreme syllables, making a kind of pentameter, the word consisting of five letters: and this intermedial S being in the Hebrew alphabet called sin, which in the English language signifies what the Latins term *peccatum*, was urged to imply that the holy Jesus should purify us from all sin and wickedness. Thus did the pulpiteer cant, while all the congregation, especially the brotherhood of divines, were so surprised at his odd way of preaching, that wonder served them, as grief did Niobe, almost turned them into stones. I among the rest (as Horace describes Priapus viewing the enchantments of the two sorceresses, Canidia and Sagane) could no longer contain, but let fly a cracking report of the operation it had upon me. These impertinent introductions are not without reason condemned; for of old, whenever Demosthenes among the Greeks, or Tully among the Latins, began their orations with so great a digression from the matter in hand, it was always looked upon as improper and unelegant, and indeed, were such a long-fetched exordium any token of a good invention, shepherds and ploughmen might lay claim

The Monk with the Sacred Hood.

to the title of men of greatest parts, since upon any argument it is easiest for them to talk what is least to the purpose. These preachers think their preamble (as we may well term it), to be the most fashionable, when it is farthest from the subject they propose to treat of, while each auditor sits and wonders what they drive at, and many times mutters out the complaint of Virgil:

Whither does all this jargon tend?

In the third place, when they come to the division of their text, they shall give only a very short touch at the interpretation of the words, when the fuller explication of their sense ought to have been their only province. Fourthly, after they are a little entered, they shall start some theological queries, far enough off from the matter in hand, and bandy it about pro and con till they lose it in the heat of scuffle. And here they shall cite their doctors invincible, subtle, seraphic, cherubic, holy, irrefragable, and such like great names to confirm their several assertions. Then out they bring their syllogisms, their majors, their minors, conclusions, corollaries, suppositions, and distinctions, that will sooner terrify the congregation into an amazement, than persuade them into a conviction. Now comes the fifth act, in which they must exert their utmost skill to come off with applause. Here therefore they fall a telling some sad lamentable story out of their legend, or some other fabulous history, and this they descant upon allegorically, tropologically, and analogically; and so they draw to a conclusion of their discourse, which is a more brain-sick chimera than ever Horace could describe in his *De Arte Poetica*, when he began:

Humano Capiti, &c.

Their praying is altogether as ridiculous as their preaching; for imagining that in their addresses to heaven they should set out in a low and tremulous voice, as a token of dread and reverence, they begin therefore with such a soft whispering as if they were afraid anyone should overhear what they said; but when they are gone a little way, they clear up their pipes by degrees, and at last bawl out so loud as if, with Baal's priests, they were resolved to awake a sleeping god; and then again, being told by rhetoricians that heights and falls, and a different cadency in pronunciation, is a great advantage to the setting off anything that is spoken, they

Bell and the Dragon.

will sometimes as it were mutter their words inwardly, and then of a sudden hollo them out, and be sure at last, in such a flat, faltering tone as if their spirits were spent, and they had run themselves out of breath. Lastly, they have read that most systems of rhetoric treat of the art of exciting laughter; therefore for the effecting of this they will sprinkle some jests and puns that must pass for ingenuity, though they are only the froth and folly of affectedness. Sometimes they will nibble at the wit of being satyrical, though their utmost spleen is so toothless, that they suck rather than bite, tickle rather than scratch or wound: nor do they ever flatter more than at such times as they pretend to speak with greatest freedom.

Finally, all their actions are so buffoonish and mimical, that any would judge they had learned all their tricks of mountebanks and stage-players, who in action it is true may perhaps outdo them, but in oratory there is so little odds between both, that it is hard to determine which seems of longest standing in the schools of eloquence. Yet these preachers, however ridiculous, meet with such hearers, who admire them as much as the people of Athens did Demosthenes, or the citizens of Rome could do Cicero: among which admirers are chiefly shopkeepers, and women, whose approbation and good opinion they only court; because the first, if they are humoured, give them some snacks out of unjust gain; and the last come and ease their grief to them upon all pinching occasions, especially when their husbands are any ways cross or unkind.

Thus much I suppose may suffice to make you sensible how much these cell-hermits and recluses are indebted to my bounty; who when they tyrannize over the consciences of the deluded laity with fopperies, juggles, and impostures, yet think themselves as eminently pious as St. Paul, St. Anthony, or any other of the saints; but these stage-divines, not less ungrateful disowners of their obligations to folly, than they are impudent pretenders to the profession of piety, I willingly take my leave of, and pass now to kings, princes, and courtiers, who paying me a devout acknowledgment, may justly challenge back the respect of being mentioned and taken notice of by me. And first, had they wisdom enough to make a true judgment of things, they would find their own condition to be more despicable and slavish than that of the most menial subjects. For certainly none can esteem perjury or parricide a cheap purchase for a crown, if he does but seriously reflect on that weight of cares a princely diadem is loaded with. He that sits at the helm of government acts in a public capacity, and so must sacrifice all private interest to the attainment of the

King David.

common good; he must himself be conformable to those laws his prerogative exacts, or else he can expect no obedience paid them from others; he must have a strict eye over all his inferior magistrates and officers, or otherwise it is to be doubted they will but carelessly discharge their respective duties. Every king, within his own territories, is placed for a shining example as it were in the firmament of his widespread dominions, to prove either a glorious star of benign influence, if his behaviour be remarkably just and innocent, or else to impend as a threatening comet, if his blazing power be pestilent and hurtful. Subjects move in a darker sphere, and so their wanderings and failings are less discernible; whereas princes, being fixed in a more exalted orb, and encompassed with a brighter dazzling lustre, their spots are more apparently visible, and their eclipses, or other defects, influential on all that is inferior to them. Kings are baited with so many temptations and opportunities to vice and immorality, such as are high feeding, liberty, flattery, luxury, and the like, that they must stand perpetually on their guard, to fence off those assaults that are always ready to be made upon them. In fine, abating from treachery, hatred, dangers, fear, and a thousand other mischiefs impending on crowned heads, however uncontrollable they are this side heaven, yet after their reign here they must appear before a supremer judge, and there be called to an exact account for the discharge of that great stewardship which was committed to their trust. If princes did but seriously consider (and consider they would if they were but wise) these many hardships of a royal life, they would be so perplexed in the result of their thoughts thereupon, as scarce to eat or sleep in quiet. But now by my assistance they leave all these cares to the gods, and mind only their own ease and pleasure, and therefore will admit none to their attendance but who will divert them with sport and mirth, lest they should otherwise be seized and damped with the surprisal of sober thoughts. They think they have sufficiently acquitted themselves in the duty of governing, if they do but ride constantly a hunting, breed up good race-horses, sell places and offices to those of the courtiers that will give most for them, and find out new ways for invading of their people's property, and hooking in a larger revenue to their own exchequer; for the procurement whereof they will always have some pretended claim and title; that though it be manifest extortion, yet it may bear the show of law and justice: and then they daub over their oppression with a submissive, flattering carriage, that they may so far insinuate into the affections of the vulgar, as they may not tumult nor rebel, but patiently crouch to burdens and exactions. Let us feign now a person

ignorant of the laws and constitutions of that realm he lives in, an enemy
to the public good, studious only for his own private interest, addicted
wholly to pleasures and delights, a hater of learning, a professed enemy
to liberty and truth, careless and unmindful of the common concerns,
taking all the measures of justice and honesty from the false beam of self-
interest and advantage, after this hang about his neck a gold chain, for
an intimation that he ought to have all virtues linked together; then set
a crown of gold and jewels on his head, for a token that he ought to over-
top and outshine others in all commendable qualifications; next, put into
his hand a royal sceptre for a symbol of justice and integrity; lastly, clothe
him with purple, for an hieroglyphic of a tender love and affection to the
commonwealth. If a prince should look upon this portraiture, and draw
a comparison between that and himself, certainly he would be ashamed
of his ensigns of majesty, and be afraid of being laughed out of them.

Next to kings themselves may come their courtiers, who, though they
are for the most part a base, servile, cringing, low-spirited sort of flatterers,
yet they look big, swell great, and have high thoughts of their honour and
grandeur. Their confidence appears upon all occasions; yet in this one
thing they are very modest, in that they are content to adorn their bodies
with gold, jewels, purple, and other glorious ensigns of virtue and wisdom,
but leave their minds empty and unfraught; and taking the resemblance
of goodness to themselves, turn over the truth and reality of it to others.
They think themselves mighty happy in that they can call the king master,
and be allowed the familiarity of talking with him; that they can volubly
rehearse his several titles of august highness, supereminent excellence,
and most serene majesty, that they can boldly usher in any discourse, and
that they have the complete knack of insinuation and flattery; for these
are the arts that make them truly genteel and noble. If you make a stricter
enquiry after their other endowments, you shall find them mere sots
and dolts. They will sleep generally till noon, and then their mercenary
chaplains shall come to their bedside, and entertain them perhaps with a
short morning prayer. As soon as they are drest they must go to breakfast,
and when that is done, immediately to dinner. When the cloth is taken
away, then to cards, dice, tables, or some such like diversion. After this
they must have one or two afternoon banquets, and so in the evening to
supper. When they have supped then begins the game of drinking; the
bottles are marshalled, the glasses ranked, and round go the healths and
bumpers till they are carried to bed. And this is the constant method of
passing away their hours, days, months, years, and ages. I have many times

The Sovereign.

took great satisfaction by standing in the court, and seeing how the tawdry butterflies vie upon one another: the ladies shall measure the height of their humours by the length of their trails, which must be borne up by a page behind. The nobles justle one another to get nearest to the king's elbow, and wear gold chains of that weight and bigness as require no less strength to carry than they do wealth to purchase.

And now for some reflections upon popes, cardinals, and bishops, who in pomp and splendour have almost equalled if not outgone secular princes. Now if anyone consider that their upper crotchet of white linen is to signify their unspotted purity and innocence; that their forked mitres, with both divisions tied together by the same knot, are to denote the joint knowledge of the Old and New Testament; that their always wearing gloves represents their keeping their hands clean and undefiled from lucre and covetousness; that the pastoral staff implies the care of a flock committed to their charge; that the cross carried before them expresses their victory over all carnal affections; he (I say) that considers this, and much more of the like nature, must needs conclude they are entrusted with a very weighty and difficult office. But alas, they think it sufficient if they can but feed themselves; and as to their flock, either commend them to the care of Christ himself, or commit them to the guidance of some inferior vicars and curates; not so much as remembering what their name of bishop imports, to wit, labour, pains, and diligence, but by base simoniacal contracts, they are in a profane sense *Episcopi*, i.e., overseers of their own gain and income.

So cardinals, in like manner, if they did but consider that the church supposes them to succeed in the room of the apostles; that therefore they must behave themselves as their predecessors, and so not be lords, but dispensers of spiritual gifts, of the disposal whereof they must one day render a strict account: or if they would but reflect a little on their habit, and thus reason with themselves, what means this white upper garment, but only an unspotted innocence? What signifies my inner purple, but only an ardent love and zeal to God? What imports my outermost pall, so wide and long that it covers the whole mule when I ride, nay, should be big enough to cover a camel, but only a diffusive charity, that should spread itself for a succour and protection to all, by teaching, exhorting, comforting, reproving, admonishing, composing of differences, courageously withstanding wicked princes, and sacrificing for the safety of our flock our life and blood, as well as our wealth and riches; though indeed riches ought not to be at all possessed by such as boast themselves successors to the apostles, who were poor, needy, and destitute: I say, if they did but lay these considerations to heart they would never be so ambitious of being created to this honour, they would willingly resign it when conferred upon them, or at least would be as industrious, watchful and laborious, as the primitive apostles were.

Now as to the popes of Rome, who pretend themselves Christ's vicars, if they would but imitate his exemplary life, in the being employed in an unintermitted course of preaching; in the being attended with poverty, nakedness, hunger, and a contempt of this world; if they did but consider the import of the word pope, which signifies a father; or if they did but practice their surname of most holy, what order or degrees of men would be in a worse condition? There would be then no such vigorous making of parties, and buying of votes, in the conclave upon a vacancy of that see: and those who by bribery, or other indirect courses, should get themselves elected, would never secure their sitting firm in the chair by pistol, poison, force, and violence. How much of their pleasure would be abated if they were but endowed with one dram of wisdom? Wisdom, did I say? Nay, with one grain of that salt which our Saviour bid them not lose the savour of. All their riches, all their honour, their jurisdictions, their Peter's patrimony, their offices, their dispensations, their licences, their indulgences, their long train and attendants (see in how short a compass I have abbreviated all their marketing of religion); in a word, all their perquisites would be forfeited and lost; and in their room would succeed watchings, fastings, tears, prayers, sermons, hard studies, repenting sighs, and a thousand such like severe penalties: nay, what's yet more deplorable, it would then follow, that all their clerks, amanuenses, notaries, advocates, proctors, secretaries, the offices of grooms, ostlers, serving-men, pimps (and somewhat else, which for modesty's sake I shall not mention); in short, all these troops of attendants, which depend on his holiness, would all lose their several employments. This indeed would be hard, but what yet remains would be more dreadful: the very Head of the Church, the spiritual prince, would then be brought from all his splendour to the poor equipage of a scrip and staff. But all this is upon the supposition only that they understood what circumstances they are placed in; whereas now, by a wholesome neglect of thinking, they live as well as heart can wish: whatever of toil and drudgery belongs to their office that they assign over to St. Peter, or St. Paul, who have time enough to mind it; but if there be anything of pleasure and grandeur, that they assume to themselves, as being hereunto

Searching the Scriptures.

called: so that by my influence no sort of people live more to their own ease and content. They think to satisfy that Master they pretend to serve, our Lord and Saviour, with their great state and magnificence, with the ceremonies of instalments, with the titles of reverence and holiness, and with exercising their episcopal function only in blessing and cursing. The working of miracles is old and outdated; to teach the people is too laborious; to interpret scripture is to invade the prerogative of the schoolmen; to pray is too idle; to shed tears is cowardly and unmanly; to fast is too mean and sordid; to be easy and familiar is beneath the grandeur of him, who, without being sued to and intreated, will scarce give princes the honour of kissing his toe; finally, to die for religion is too self-denying; and to be crucified as their Lord of Life, is base and ignominious. Their only weapons ought to be those of the Spirit; and of these indeed they are mighty liberal, as of their interdicts, their suspensions, their denunciations, their aggravations, their greater and lesser excommunications, and their roaring bulls, that fright whomever they are thundered against; and these most holy fathers never issue them out more frequently than against those, who, at the instigation of the devil, and not having the fear of God before their eyes, do feloniously and maliciously attempt to lessen and impair St. Peter's patrimony: and though that apostle tells our Saviour in the gospel, in the name of all the other disciples, we have left all, and followed you, yet they challenge as his inheritance, fields, towns, treasures, and large dominions; for the defending whereof, inflamed with a holy zeal, they fight with fire and sword, to the great loss and effusion of Christian blood, thinking they are apostolical maintainers of Christ's spouse, the church, when they have murdered all such as they call her enemies; though indeed the church has no enemies more bloody and tyrannical than such impious popes, who give dispensations for the not preaching of Christ; evacuate the main effect and design of our redemption by their pecuniary bribes and sales; adulterate the gospel by their forced interpretations, and undermining traditions; and lastly, by their lusts and wickedness grieve the Holy Spirit, and make their Saviour's wounds to bleed anew. Farther, when the Christian church has been all along first planted, then confirmed, and since established by the blood of her martyrs, as if Christ her head would be wanting in the same methods still of protecting her, they invert the order, and propagate their religion now by arms and violence, which was wont formerly to be done only with patience and sufferings. And though war be so brutish, as that it becomes beasts rather than men; so extravagant, that the poets feigned it an effect of the furies; so licentious, that it stops the course of all justice and honesty, so desperate, that it is best waged by ruffians and banditti, and so unchristian, that it is contrary to the express commands of the gospel; yet maugre all this, peace is too quiet, too inactive, and they must be engaged in the boisterousness of war. Among which undertaking popes, you shall have some so old that they can scarce creep, and yet they will put on a young, brisk resolution, will resolve to stick at no pains, to spare no cost, nor to waive any inconvenience, so they may involve laws, religion, peace, and all other concerns, whether sacred or civil, in unappeasable tumults and distractions. And yet some of their learned fawning courtiers will interpret this notorious madness for zeal, and piety, and fortitude, having found out the way how a man may draw his sword, and sheathe it in his brother's bowels, and yet not offend against the duty of the second table, whereby we are obliged to love our neighbours as ourselves. It is yet uncertain whether these Romish fathers have taken example from, or given precedent to, such other German bishops, who omitting their ecclesiastical habit, and other ceremonies, appear openly armed cap-a-pie, like so many champions and warriors, thinking no doubt that they come short of the duty of their function, if they die in any other place than the open field, fighting the battles of the Lord. The inferior clergy, deeming it unmannerly not to conform to their patrons and diocesans, devoutly tug and fight for their tithes with syllogisms and arguments, as fiercely as with swords, sticks, stones, or anything that came next to hand. When they read the rabbies, fathers, or other ancient writings, how quick-sighted are they in spying out any sentences, that they may frighten the people with, and make them believe that more than the tenth is due, passing by whatever they meet with in the same authors that minds them of the duty and difficulty of their own office. They never consider that their shaven crown is a token that they should pare off and cut away all the superfluous lusts of this world, and give themselves wholly to divine meditation; but instead of this, our bald-pated priests think they have done enough, if they do but mumble over such a fardel of prayers; which it is a wonder if God should hear or understand, when they whisper them so softly, and in so unknown a language, which they can scarce hear or understand themselves. This they have in common with other mechanics, that they are most subtle in the craft of getting money, and wonderfully skilled in their respective dues of tithes, offerings, perquisites, &c. Thus they are all content to reap the profit, but as to the burden, that they toss as a ball from one hand to another, and assign it over to any they can get or hire: for as secular

The Bishop.

The Cardinal.

princes have their judges and subordinate ministers to act in their name, and supply their stead; so ecclesiastical governors have their deputies, vicars, and curates, nay, many times turn over the whole care of religion to the laity. The laity, supposing they have nothing to do with the church (as if their baptismal vow did not initiate them members of it), make it over to the priests; of the priests again, those that are secular, thinking their title implies them to be a little too profane, assign this task over to the regulars, the regulars to the monks, the monks bandy it from one order to another, till it light upon the mendicants; they lay it upon the carthusians, which order alone keeps honesty and piety among them, but really keep them so close that no body ever yet could see them. Thus the Popes thrusting only their sickle into the harvest of profit, leave all the other toil of spiritual husbandry to the bishops, the bishops bestow it upon the pastors, the pastors on their curates, and the curates commit it to the mendicants, who return it again to such as well know how to make good advantage of the flock, by the benefit of their fleece.

But I would not be thought purposely to expose the weaknesses of popes and priests, lest I should seem to recede from my title, and make a satire instead of a panegyric: nor let anyone imagine that I reflect on good princes, by commending of bad ones: I did this only in brief, to shew that there is no one particular person can lead a comfortable life, except he be entered of my society, and retain me for his friend. Nor indeed can it be otherwise, since fortune, that empress of the world, is so much in league and amity with me, that to wise men she is always stingy, and sparing of her gifts, but is profusely liberal and lavish to fools. Thus Timotheus, the Athenian commander, in all his expeditions, was a mirror of good luck, because he was a little underwitted; from him was occasioned the Grecian proverb, Ἡ εὕδοντος κύρτος ἀιρει, *The net fills, though the fisherman sleeps*; there is also another favourable proverb, γλαὺξ ἵπταται, *The owl flies*, an omen of success. But against wise men are pointed these ill-aboding proverbs, Ἐν τετράδι γεννηθέντας, *Born under a bad planet*; *equum habet seianum*, *He cannot ride the forehorse*; *aurum tholosanum*, *Ill-gotten goods will never prosper*; and more to the same purpose. But I forbear from any farther proverbializing, lest I should be thought to have rifled my Erasmus' *adages*. To return, therefore, fortune we find still favouring the blunt, and flushing the forward; strokes and smoothes up fools, crowning all their undertakings with success; but wisdom makes her followers bashful, sneaking, and timorous, and therefore you see that they are commonly reduced

Fingering Money through a Thick Pair of Gloves.

The Threatenings of the Church.

to hard shifts, must grapple with poverty, cold and hunger, must lie recluse, despised, and unregarded, while fools roll in money, are advanced to dignities and offices, and in a word, have the whole world at command. If anyone think it happy to be a favourite at court, and to manage the disposal of places and preferments, alas, this happiness is so far from being attainable by wisdom, that the very suspicion of it would put a stop to all advancement. Has any man a mind to raise himself a good estate? Alas what dealer in the world would ever get a farthing, if he be so wise as to scruple at perjury, blush at a lie, or stick at any fraud and overreaching. Farther, does anyone appear a candidate for any ecclesiastical dignity? Why, an ass, or a plough-jobber, shall sooner gain it than a wise man. Again, are you in love with any handsome lady? Alas, women-kind are so addicted to folly, that they will not at all listen to the courtship of a wise suitor. Finally, wherever there is any preparation made for mirth and jollity, all wise men are sure to be excluded the company, lest they should stint the joy, and damp the frolic. In a word, to what side soever we turn ourselves, to popes, princes, judges, magistrates, friends, enemies, rich or poor, all their concerns are managed by money, which because it is undervalued by wise men, therefore, in revenge to be sure, it never comes at them.

But now, though my praise and commendation might well be endless, yet it is requisite I should put some period to my speech. I'll therefore draw toward an end, when I have first confirmed what I have said by the authority of several authors. Which by way of farther proof I shall insist upon, partly, that I may not be thought to have said more in my own behalf than what will be justified by others; and partly, that the lawyers may not check me for citing no precedents nor allegations. To imitate them therefore I will produce some reports and authorities, though perhaps like theirs too, they are nothing to the purpose.

First then, it is confessed almost to a proverb, that the art of dissembling is a very necessary accomplishment; and therefore it is a common verse among schoolboys:

To feign the fool when fit occasions rise,
Argues the being more completely wise.

It is easy therefore to collect how great a value ought to be put upon real folly, when the very shadow, and bare imitation of it, is so much esteemed. Horace, who in his epistles thus styles himself:

My sleek-skinn'd corpse as smooth as if I lie
'Mong th' fatted swine of Epicurus' sty.

This poet (I say) gives this advice in one of his odes:

Short Folly with your counsels mix.

The epithet of short, it is true, is a little improper. The same poet again
has this passage elsewhere:

Well-timed Folly has a sweet relish.

And in another place:

I'd rather much he censured for a fool,
Than feel the lash and smart of wisdom's school.

Homer praises Telemachus as much as anyone of his heroes, and yet he
gives him the epithet of Νήπιος, *Silly:* and the Grecians generally use the
same word to express children, as a token of their innocence. And what is
the argument of all Homer's Iliads, but only, as Horace observes:

They kings and subjects dotages contain?

How positive also is Tully's commendation that all places are filled with
fools? Now every excellence being to be measured by its extent, the goodness of folly must be of as large compass as those universal places she
reaches to. But perhaps Christians may slight the authority of a heathen.
I could therefore, if I pleased, back and confirm the truth hereof by the
citations of several texts of scripture; though herein it were perhaps my
duty to beg leave of the divines, that I might so far intrench upon their
prerogative. Supposing a grant, the task seems so difficult as to require the
invocation of some aid and assistance; yet because it is unreasonable to
put the muses to the trouble and expense of so tedious a journey, especially since the business is out of their sphere, I shall choose rather (while
I am acting the divine, and venturing in their polemic difficulties), to wish
myself for such time animated with Scotus, his bristling and prickly soul,
which I would not care how afterwards it returned to his body, though

Religion turned over to the Care of the Laity.

All Concerns Arranged with Money.

for refinement it were stopped at a purgatory by the way. I cannot but wish that I might wholly change my character, or at least that some grave divine, in my stead, might rehearse this part of the subject for me; for truly I suspect that somebody will accuse me of plundering the closets of those reverend men, while I pretend to so much divinity, as must appear in my following discourse. Yet however, it may not seem strange, that after so long and frequent a converse, I have gleaned some scraps from the divines; since Horace's wooden god by hearing his master read Homer, learned some words of Greek; and Lucian's cock, by long attention, could readily understand what any man spoke. But now to the purpose, wishing myself success.

Ecclesiastes doth somewhere confess that there are an infinite number of fools. Now when he speaks of an infinite number, what does he else but imply, that herein is included the whole race of mankind, except some very few, which I know not whether ever anyone had yet the happiness to see?

The prophet Jeremiah speaks yet more plainly in his tenth chapter, where he saith, that *Every man is brutish in his knowledge*. He just before attributes wisdom to God alone, saying, that the *Wise men of the nations are altogether brutish and foolish*. And in the preceding chapter he gives this seasonable caution, *Let not the wise man glory in his wisdom*: the reason is obvious, because no man hath truly any whereof to glory. But to return to Ecclesiastes, when he saith, *Vanity of vanities, all is vanity*, what else can we imagine his meaning to be, than that our whole life is nothing but one continued interlude of Folly? This confirms that assertion of Tully, which is delivered in that noted passage we but just now mentioned, namely, that *All places swarm with fools*. Farther, what does the son of Sirach mean when he saith in Ecclesiasticus, that the *Fool is changed as the moon*, while the *Wise man is fixed as the sun*, than only to hint out the folly of all mankind; and that the name of wise is due to no other but the all-wise God? For all interpreters by Moon understand mankind, and by Sun that fountain of all light, the Almighty. The same sense is implied in that saying of our Saviour in the gospel, *There is none good but one, that is God*: for if whoever is not wise must be consequently a fool, and if, according to the Stoics, every man be wise so far only as he is good, the meaning of the text must be, all mortals are unavoidably fools; and there is none wise but one, that is God. Solomon also in the fifteenth chapter of his proverbs hath this expression, *Folly is joy to him that is destitute of wisdom*; plainly intimating, that the wise man is attended with grief and vexation, while the foolish only roll in delight and pleasure. To the same purpose is that saying of his in the first chapter of Eccleslastes, *In much wisdom is much grief; and he that increaseth knowledge increaseth sorrow.* Again, it is confessed by the same preacher in the seventh chapter of the same book, *That the heart of the wise is in the house of mourning, but the heart of fools is in the house of mirth.* This author himself had never attained to such a portion of wisdom, if he had not applied himself to a searching out the frailties and infirmities of human nature; as, if you believe not me, may appear from his own words in his first chapter, *I gave my heart to know wisdom, and to know madness and folly;* where it is worthy to be observed that as to the order of words, Folly for its advantage is put in the last place. Thus Ecclesiastes wrote, and thus indeed did an ecclesiastical method require; namely, that what has the precedence in dignity should come hindmost in rank and order, according to the tenor of that evangelical precept, *The last shall be first, and the first shall be last.* And in Ecclesiasticus likewise (whoever was author of the holy book which bears that name) in the forty-fourth chapter, the excellency of folly above wisdom is positively acknowledged; the very words I shall not cite, till I have the advantage of an answer to a question I am proposing, this way of interrogating being frequently made use of by Plato in his dialogues between Socrates, and other disputants: I ask you then, what is it we usually hoard and lock up, things of greater esteem and value, or those which are more common, trite, and despicable? Why are you so backward in making an answer? Since you are so shy and reserved, I'll take the Greek proverb for a satisfactory reply; namely, τὴν ἐπὶ θύραις ὑδρίαν, *Foul water is thrown down the sink;* which saying, that no person may slight it, may be convenient to advertise that it comes from no meaner an author than that oracle of truth, Aristotle himself. And indeed there is no one on this side Bedlam so mad as to throw out upon the dunghill his gold and jewels, but rather all persons have a close repository to preserve them in, and secure them under all the locks, bolts, and bars, that either art can contrive, or fears suggest: whereas the dirt, pebbles, and oyster-shells, that lie scattered in the streets, ye trample upon, pass by, and take no notice of. If then what is more valuable be coffered up, and what less so lies unregarded, it follows, that accordingly Folly should meet with a greater esteem than wisdom, because that wise author advises us to the keeping close and concealing the first, and exposing or laying open the other: as take him now in his own words, *Better is he that hideth his folly than him that*

The Courtier.

The Brutish Man.

hideth his wisdom. Beside, the sacred text does oft ascribe innocence and sincerity to fools, while the wise man is apt to be a haughty scorner of all such as he thinks or censures to have less wit than himself: for so I understand that passage in the tenth chapter of Ecclesiastes, *When he that is a fool walketh by the way, his wisdom faileth him, and he saith to everyone that he is a fool.* Now what greater argument of candour or ingenuity can there be, than to demean himself equal with all others, and not think their deserts any way inferior to his own. Folly is no such scandalous attribute, but that the wise Agur was not ashamed to confess it, in the thirtieth chapter of Proverbs: *Surely I am more brutish than any man, and have not the understanding of a man.* Nay, St. Paul himself, that great doctor of the Gentiles, writing to his Corinthians, readily owns the name, saying, *If any man speak as a fool, I am more;* as if to have been less so had been a reproach and disgrace. But perhaps I may be censured for misinterpreting this text by some modern annotators, who like crows pecking at one another's eyes, find fault, and correct all that went before them, pretend each their own glosses to contain the only true and genuine explication; among whom my Erasmus (whom I cannot but mention with respect) may challenge the second place, if not the precedency. This citation (say they) is purely impertinent; the meaning of the apostle is far different from what you dream of: he would not have these words so understood, as if he desired to be thought a greater fool than the rest, but only when he had before said, *Are they ministers of Christ? So am I:* as if the equalling himself herein to others had been too little, he adds, *I am more,* thinking a bare equality not enough, unless he were even superior to those he compares himself with. This he would have to be believed as true; yet lest it might be thought offensive, as bordering too much on arrogance and conceit, he tempers and alleviates it by the covert of Folly. *I speak* (says he) *as a fool,* knowing it to be the peculiar privilege of fools to speak the truth, without giving offence. But what St. Paul's thoughts were when he wrote this, I leave for them to determine. In my own judgment at least I prefer the opinion of the good old tunbellied divines, with whom it's safer and more creditable to err, than to be in the right with smattering, raw, novices.

Nor indeed should anyone mind the late critics any more than the senseless chattering of a daw: especially since one of the most eminent of them (whose name I advisedly conceal, lest some of our wits should be taunting him with the Greek proverb, Ὄνος πρὸς λύραν, *ad lyram asinus*) magisterially and dogmatically descanting upon his text [*are they the*

All is Vanity.

ministers of Christ? *(I speak as a fool) I am more]* makes a distinct chapter, and (which without good store of logic he could never have done) adds a new section, and then gives this paraphrase, which I shall verbatim recite, that you may have his words materially, as well as formally his sense (for that's one of their babbling distinctions). *[I speak as a fool]* that is, if the equalling myself to those false apostles would have been construed as the vaunt of a fool, I will willingly be accounted a greater fool, by taking place of them, and openly pleading, that as to their ministry, I not only come up even with them, but outstrip and go beyond them: though this same commentator a little after, as it were forgetting what he had just before delivered, tacks about and shifts to another interpretation.

But why do I insist upon anyone particular example, when in general it is the public charter of all divines, to mould and bend the sacred oracles till they comply with their own fancy, spreading them (as Heaven by its Creator) like a curtain, closing together, or drawing them back, as they please? Thus indeed St. Paul himself minces and mangles some citations he makes use of, and seems to wrest them to a different sense from what they were first intended for, as is confessed by the great linguist, St. Hierom. Thus when that apostle saw at Athens the inscription of an altar, he draws from it an argument for the proof of the christian religion; but leaving out great part of the sentence, which perhaps if fully recited might have prejudiced his cause, he mentions only the two last words viz., *To the unknown God;* and this too not without alteration, for the whole inscription runs thus: *To the Gods of* Asia, Europe, *and* Africa, *to all foreign and unknown Gods.*

'Tis an imitation of the same pattern, I will warrant you, that our young divines, by leaving out four or five words in a place, and putting a false construction on the rest, can make any passage serviceable to their own purpose; though from the coherence of what went before, or follows after, the genuine meaning appears to be either wide enough, or perhaps quite contradictory to what they would thrust and impose upon it. In which knack the divines are grown now so expert, that the lawyers themselves begin to be jealous of an encroachment upon what was formerly their sole privilege and practice. And indeed what can they despair of proving, since the fore-mentioned commentator (I had almost blundered out his name), but that I am restrained by fear of the same Greek proverbial sarcasm) did upon a text of St. Luke put an interpretation, no more agreeable to the meaning of the place, than one contrary quality is to another? The

The Devotion to Folly.

The Prophet Jeremiah.

passage is this, when Judas' treachery was preparing to be executed, and accordingly it seemed requisite that all the disciples should be provided to guard and secure their assaulted master, our Saviour, that he might piously caution them against reliance for his delivery on any worldly strength, asks them, whether in all their embassy they lacked anything, when he had sent them out so unfurnished for the performance of a long journey, that they had not so much as shoes to defend their feet from the injuries of flints and thorns, or a scrip to carry a meal's meat in; and when they had answered that they lacked nothing, he adds, *But now he that hath a purse let him take it, and likewise a scrip; and he that hath no sword let him sell his garment, and buy one.* Now when the whole doctrine of our Saviour inculcates nothing more frequently than meekness, patience, and a contempt of this world, is it not plain what the meaning of the place is? Namely, that he might now dismiss his ambassadors in a more naked, defenceless condition, he does not only advise them to take no thought for shoes or scrip, but even commands them to part with the very clothes from their back, that so they might have the less incumbrance and entanglement in the going through their office and function. He cautions them, it is true, to be furnished with a sword, yet not such a carnal one as rogues and highwaymen make use of for murder and bloodshed, but with the sword of the Spirit, which pierces through the heart, and searches out the innermost retirements of the soul, lopping off all our lust, and corrupt affections, and leaving nothing in possession of our breast but piety, zeal, and devotion: this (I say) in my opinion is the most natural interpretation. But see how that divine misunderstands the place; by sword (says he) is meant, defence against persecution; by scrip, or purse, a sufficient quantity of provision; as if Christ had, by considering better of it, changed his mind in reference to that mean equipage, which he had before sent his disciples in, and therefore came now to a recantation of what he had formerly instituted: or as if he had forgot what in time past he had told them, *Blessed are you when men shall revile you, and persecute you, and say all manner of evil against you for my sake. Render not evil for evil,* for *blessed are the meek,* not the cruel: as if he had forgot that he encouraged them by the examples of sparrows and lilies to take no thought for the morrow; he gives them now another lesson, and charges them, rather than go *without a sword, to sell their garment, and buy one;* as if the going cold and naked were more excusable than the marching unarmed. And as this author thinks all means which are requisite for the prevention or retaliation of injuries to be implied under the name of sword, so under that of scrip, he would have everything to be comprehended, which either the necessity or conveniency of life requires.

Thus does this provident commentator furnish out the disciples with halberts, spears, and guns, for the enterprise of preaching Christ crucified; he supplies them at the same time with pockets, bags, and portmanteaus, that they might carry their cupboards as well as their bellies always about them: he takes no notice how our Saviour afterwards rebukes Peter for drawing that sword which he had just before so strictly charged him to buy; nor that it is ever recorded that the primitive christians did by no ways withstand their heathen persecutors otherwise than with tears and prayers, which they would have exchanged more effectually for swords and bucklers, if they had thought this text would have borne them out.

There is another, and he of no mean credit, whom for respect to his person I shall forbear to name, who commenting upon that verse in the prophet Habakkuk (*I saw the tents of Cushan in affliction, and the curtains of the land of Midian did tremble*), because tents were sometimes made of skins, he pretended that the word tents did here signify the skin of St. Bartholomew, who was flayed for a martyr.

I myself was lately at a divinity disputation (where I very often pay my attendance), where one of the opponents demanded a reason why it should be thought more proper to silence all heretics by sword and faggot, rather than convert them by moderate and sober arguments? A certain cynical old blade, who bore the character of a divine, legible in the frowns and wrinkles of his face, not without a great deal of disdain answered, that it was the express injunction of St. Paul himself, in those directions to Titus (*A man that is an heretic, after the first and second admonition, reject*), quoting it in Latin, where the word *reject* is *devita*, while all the auditory wondered at this citation, and deemed it no way applicable to his purpose; he at last explained himself, saying, that *devita* signified *de vita tollendum hereticum*, a heretic must be slain. Some smiled at his ignorance, but others approved of it as an orthodox comment. And however some disliked that such violence should be done to so easy a text, our hairsplitting and irrefragable doctor went on in triumph. To prove it yet (says he) more undeniably, it is commanded in the old law [*Thou shalt not suffer a witch to live*]: now then every *Maleficus*, or witch, is to be killed, but an heretic is *Maleficus*, which in the Latin translation is put for a witch, *ergo, &c.* All that were present wondered at the ingenuity of the person, and very devoutly embraced his opinion, never dreaming that the law was restrained only to magicians, sorcerers, and enchanters: for otherwise,

The Pope.

if the word *Maleficus* signified what it most naturally implies, every evildoer, then drunkenness and whoredom were to meet with the same capital punishment as witchcraft. But why should I squander away my time in a too tedious prosecution of this topic, which if drove on to the utmost would afford talk to eternity? I aim herein at no more than this, namely, that since those grave doctors take such a swinging range and latitude, I, who am but a smattering novice in divinity, may have the larger allowance for any slips or mistakes.

Now therefore I return to St. Paul, who uses these expressions [*Ye suffer fools gladly*], applying it to himself; and again [*As a fool receive me*], and [*That which I speak, I speak not after the Lord, but as it were foolishly*]; and in another place [*We are fools for Christ's sake*]. See how these commendations of Folly are equal to the author of them, both great and sacred. The same holy person does yet enjoin and command the being a fool, as a virtue of all others most requisite and necessary: for, says he [*If any man seem to be wise in this world, let him become a fool, that he may be wise*]. Thus St. Luke records, how our Saviour, after his resurrection, joining himself with two of his disciples travelling to Emmaus, at his first salutation he calls them fools, saying [*O fools, and slow of heart to believe*]. Nor may this seem strange in comparison to what is yet farther delivered by St. Paul, who adventures to attribute something of Folly even to the all-wise God himself [*The foolishness of God* (says he) *is wiser than men*]; in which text St. Origen would not have the word foolishness any way referred to men, or applicable to the same sense, wherein is to be understood that other passage of St. Paul [*The preaching of the cross to them that perish, foolishness*]. But why do I put myself to the trouble of citing so many proofs, since this one may suffice for all, namely, that in those mystical psalms wherein David represents the type of Christ, it is there acknowledged by our Saviour, in way of confession, that even he himself was guilty of Folly; *Thou* (says he) *O God knowest my foolishness?* Nor is it without some reason that fools for their plainness and sincerity of heart have always been most acceptable to God Almighty. For as the princes of this world have shrewdly suspected, and carried a jealous eye over such of their subjects as were the most observant, and deepest politicians (for thus Cæsar was afraid of the plodding Cassius, and Brutus, thinking himself secure enough from the careless drinking Anthony; Nero likewise mistrusted Seneca, and Dionysius would have been willingly rid of Plato), whereas they can all put greater confidence in such as are of less subtlety and contrivance. So our Saviour in like manner dislikes and condemns the wise and crafty, as St. Paul does expressly declare in these words, *God hath chosen the foolish things of the world;* and again, *it pleased God by foolishness to save the world;* implying that by wisdom it could never have been saved. Nay, God himself testifies as much when he speaks by the mouth of his prophet, *I will destroy the wisdom of the wise, and bring to nought the understanding of the learned.* Again, our Saviour does solemnly return his Father thanks for that he had *hidden the mysteries of salvation from the wise, and revealed them to babes,* i.e., to fools; for the original word νηπίοις, being opposed to σοφοῖς, if one signify wise, the other must foolish. To the same purpose did our blessed Lord frequently condemn and upbraid the scribes, pharisees, and lawyers, while he carries himself kind and obliging to the unlearned multitude: for what otherwise can be the meaning of that tart denunciation, *Woe unto you scribes and pharisees,* than woe unto you wise men, whereas he seems chiefly delighted with children, women, and illiterate fishermen.

We may farther take notice, that among all the several kinds of brute creatures he shews greatest liking to such as are farthest distant from the subtlety of the fox. Thus in his progress to Jerusalem he chose to ride sitting upon an ass, though, if he pleased, he might have mounted the back of a lion with more of state, and as little of danger. The Holy Spirit chose rather likewise to descend from heaven in the shape of a simple gall-less dove, than that of an eagle, kite, or other more lofty fowl.

Thus all along in the holy scriptures there are frequent metaphors and similitudes of the most inoffensive creatures, such as stags, hinds, lambs, and the like. Nay, those blessed souls that in the day of judgment are to be placed at our Saviour's right hand are called sheep, which are the most senseless and stupid of all cattle, as is evidenced by Aristotle's Greek proverb, προβάτων ἦθος, a sheepishness of temper, i.e., a dull, blockish, sleepy, unmanly humour. Yet of such a flock Christ is not ashamed to profess himself the shepherd. Nay, he would not only have all his proselytes termed sheep, but even he himself would be called a lamb; as when John the Baptist seeth Jesus coming unto him, he saith, *Behold the Lamb of God;* which same title is very often given to our Saviour in the apocalypse.

All this amounts to no less than that all mortal men are fools, even the righteous and godly as well as sinners; nay, in some sense our blessed Lord himself, who, although he was *the wisdom of the Father,* yet to repair the infirmities of fallen man, he became in some measure a partaker of human Folly, when he *took our nature upon him, and was found in fashion as a man;* or when *God made him to be sin for us, who knew no sin, that we might be made the righteousness of God in him.* Nor would he heal those breaches our sins

The Provident Preacher.

Slow of Heart.

had made by any other method than by the *foolishness of the cross*, published by the ignorant and unlearned apostles, to whom he frequently recommends the excellence of Folly, cautioning them against the infectiousness of wisdom, by the several examples he proposes them to imitate, such as children, lilies, sparrows, mustard, and such like beings, which are either wholly inanimate, or at least devoid of reason and ingenuity, guided by no other conduct than that of instinct, without care, trouble, or contrivance. To the same intent the disciples were warned by their lord and master, that when they should be *brought unto the synagogues, and unto magistrates and powers*, they shall *take no thought how, or what thing they should answer, nor what they should say:* they were again strictly forbid to *enquire into the times and seasons*, or to place any confidence in their own abilities, but to depend wholly upon divine assistance.

At the first peopling of paradise the Almighty had never laid so strict a charge on our father Adam to refrain from *eating of the tree of knowledge* except he had thereby forewarned that the taste of knowledge would be the bane of all happiness. St. Paul says expressly, that *knowledge puffeth up*, i.e., it is fatal and poisonous. In pursuance whereunto St. Bernard interprets that *exceeding high mountain* whereon the devil had erected his seat to have been the mountain of knowledge. And perhaps this may be another argument which ought not to be omitted, namely, that Folly is acceptable, at least excusable, with the gods, inasmuch, as they easily pass by the heedless failures of fools, while the miscarriages of such as are known to have more wit shall very hardly obtain a pardon; nay, when a wise man comes to sue for an acquitment from any guilt, he must shroud himself under the patronage and pretext of Folly. For thus in the twelfth of Numbers Aaron entreats Moses to stay the leprosy of his sister Miriam, saying, *alas, my Lord, I beseech thee lay not the sin upon us, wherein we have done foolishly.* Thus, when David spared Saul's life, when he found him sleeping in a tent of Hachilah, not willing to *stretch forth his hand against the Lord's anointed*, Saul excuses his former severity by confessing, *Behold, I have played the fool, and have erred exceedingly.* David also himself in much the same form begs the remission of his sin from God Almighty with this prayer, *Lord, I pray thee take away the iniquity of thy servant, for I have done very foolishly;* as if he could not have hoped otherwise to have his pardon granted except he petitioned for it under the covert and mitigation of Folly. The agreeable practice of our Saviour is yet more convincing, who, when he hung upon the cross, prayed for his enemies, saying, *Father, forgive them*, urging no other plea in their behalf than that of their

Wise in the Distribution of Charity.

ignorance, *for they know not what they do.* To the same effect St. Paul in his first epistle to Timothy acknowledges he had been a blasphemer and a persecutor, *But* (saith he) *I obtained mercy, because I did it ignorantly in unbelief.* Now what is the meaning of the phrase [*I did it ignorantly*] but only this? My fault was occasioned from a misinformed Folly, not from a deliberate malice. What signifies [*I obtained mercy*] but only that I should not otherwise have obtained it had not folly and ignorance been my vindication? To the same purpose is that other passage in the mysterious Psalmist, which I forgot to mention in its proper place, namely, *Oh remember not the sins and offences of my youth!* The word which we render offences, is in Latin *ignorantias,* ignorances. Observe, the two things he alleges in his excuse are, first, his rawness of age, to which Folly and want of experience are constant attendants: and secondly, his ignorances, expressed in the plural number for an enhancement and aggravation of his foolishness.

But that I may not wear out this subject too far, to draw now towards a conclusion, it is observable that the Christian religion seems to have some relation to Folly, and no alliance at all with wisdom. Of the truth whereof, if you desire farther proof than my bare word you may please, first, to consider, that children, women, old men, and fools, led as it were by a secret impulse of nature, are always most constant in repairing to church, and most zealous, devout and attentive in the performance of the several parts of divine service; nay, the first promulgators of the gospel, and the first converts to Christinity, were men of plainness and simplicity, wholly unacquainted with secular policy or learning.

Farther, there are none more silly, or nearer their wits' end, than those who are too superstitiously religious: they are profusely lavish in their charity; they invite fresh affronts by an easy forgiveness of past injuries; they suffer themselves to be cheated and imposed upon by laying claim to the innocence of the dove; they make it the interest of no person to oblige them, because they will love, and *do good to their enemies,* as much as to the most endearing friends; they banish all pleasure, feeding upon the penance of watching, weeping, fasting, sorrow and reproach; they value not their lives, but with St. Paul, *wish to be dissolved,* and covet the fiery trial of martyrdom: in a word, they seem altogether so destitute of common sense, that their soul seems already separated from the dead and inactive body. And what else can we imagine all this to be than downright madness? It is the less strange therefore that at the feast of Pentecost the apostles should be thought drunk with new wine; or that St. Paul was censured by Festus to have been beside himself.

Industry.

And since I have had the confidence to go thus far, I shall venture yet a little forwarder, and be so bold as to say thus much more: all that final happiness, which christians, through so many rubs and briars of difficulties, contend for, is at last no better than a sort of folly and madness. This, no question, will be thought extravagantly spoke; but consider awhile, and deliberately state the case.

First, then, the christians so far agree with the Platonists as to believe that the body is no better than a prison or dungeon for the confinement of the soul. That therefore, while the soul is shackled to the walls of flesh, her soaring wings are impeded, and all her enlivening faculties clogged and fettered by the gross particles of matter, so that she can neither freely range after, nor, when happily overtook, can quietly contemplate her proper object of truth.

Farther, Plato defines philosophy to be the meditation of death, because the one performs the same office with the other; namely, withdraws the mind from all visible and corporeal objects; therefore while the soul does patiently actuate the several organs and members of the body, so long is a man accounted of a good and sound disposition; but when the soul, weary of her confinement, struggles to break jail, and fly beyond her cage of flesh and blood, then a man is censured at least for being magotty and crack-brained; nay, if there be any defect in the external organs it is then termed downright madness. And yet many times persons thus affected shall have prophetic ecstacies of foretelling things to come, shall in a rapture talk languages they never before learned, and seem in all things actuated by somewhat divine and extraordinary; and all this, no doubt, is only the effect of the soul's being more released from its engagement to the body, whereby it can with less impediment exert the energy of life and motion. From hence, no question, has sprung an observation of like nature, confirmed now into a settled opinion, that *some long experienced souls in the world, before their dislodging, arrive to the height of prophetic spirits.*

If this disorder arise from an intemperance in religion, and too high a strain of devotion, though it be of a somewhat differing sort, yet it is so near akin to the former, that a great part of mankind apprehend it as a mere madness; especially when persons of that superstitious humour are so pragmatical and singular as to separate and live apart as it were from all the world beside: so as they seem to have experienced what Plato dreams to have happened between some, who, enclosed in a dark cave, did only ruminate on the ideas and abstracted speculations of entities; and one other of their company, who had got abroad into the open light, and at his return tells them what a blind mistake they had lain under; that he had seen the substance of what their dotage of imagination reached only in shadow; that therefore he could not but pity and condole their deluding dreams, while they on the other side no less bewail his frenzy, and turn him out of their society for a lunatic and madman.

Thus the vulgar are wholly taken up with those objects that are most familiar to their senses, beyond which they are apt to think all is but fairy-land; while those that are devoutly religious scorn to set their thoughts or affections on any things below, but mount their soul to the pursuit of incorporeal and invisible beings. The former, in their marshalling the requisites of happiness, place riches in the front, the endowments of the body in the next rank, and leave the accomplishments of the soul to bring up the rear; nay, some will scarce believe there is any such thing at all as the soul, because they cannot literally see a reason of their faith; while the other pay their first fruits of service to that most simple and incomprehensible Being, God, employ themselves next in providing for the happiness of that which comes nearest to their immortal soul, being not at all mindful of their corrupt bodily carcases, and slighting money as the dirt and rubbish of the world; or if at anytime some urging occasions require them to become entangled in secular affairs, they do it with regret, and a kind of ill-will, observing what St. Paul advises his *Corinthians, having wives, and yet being as though they had none; buying, and yet remaining as though they possessed not.*

There are between these two sorts of persons many differences in several other respects. As first, though all the senses have the same mutual relation to the body, yet some are more gross than others; as those five corporeal ones, of touching, hearing, smelling, seeing, tasting, whereas some again are more refined, and less adulterated with matter; such are the memory, the understanding, and the will. Now the mind will be always most ready and expedite at that to which it is naturally most inclined. Hence is it that a pious soul, employing all its power and abilities in the pressing after such things as are farthest removed from sense, is perfectly stupid and brutish in the management of any worldly affairs; while on the other side, the vulgar are so intent upon their business and employment, that they have not time to bestow one poor thought upon a future eternity. From such ardour of divine meditation was it that Saint Bernard in his study drank oil instead of wine, and yet his thoughts were so taken up that he never observed the mistake.

Farther, among the passions of the soul, some have a greater communication with the body than others; as lust, the desire of meat and sleep, anger, pride, and envy; with these the pious man is in continual war, and irreconcileable enmity, while the vulgar cherish and foment them as the best comforts of life.

There are other affections of a middle nature, common and innate to every man; such are love to one's country, duty to parents, love to children, kindness to friends, and such like; to these the vulgar pay some respect, but the religious endeavour to supplant and eradicate from their soul, except they can raise and sublimate them to the most refined pitch of virtue; so as to love or honour their parents, not barely under that character (for what did they do more than generate a body? Nay, even for that we are primarily beholden to God, the first parent of all mankind), but as good men only, upon whom is imprinted the lively image of that divine nature, which they esteem as the chief and only good, beyond whom nothing deserves to be beloved, nothing desired.

By the same rule they measure all the other offices or duties of life; in each of which, whatever is earthly and corporeal, shall, if not wholly rejected, yet at least be put behind what faith makes the *substance of things not seen*. Thus in the sacraments, and all other acts of religion, they make a difference between the outward appearance or body of them, and the more inward soul or spirit. As to instance, in fasting, they think it very ineffectual to abstain from flesh, or debar themselves of a meal's meat (which yet is all the vulgar understand by his duty), unless they likewise restrain their passions, subdue their anger, and mortify their pride; that the soul being thus disengaged from the entanglement of the body, may have a better relish to spiritual objects, and take an antepast of heaven. Thus (say they) in the holy Eucharist, though the outward form and ceremonies are not wholly to be despised, yet are these prejudicial, at least unprofitable, if as bare signs only they are not accompanied with the thing signified, which is *the body and blood of Christ*, whose death, till his second coming, we are hereby to represent by the vanquishing and burying our vile affections that they may arise to a newness of life, and be united first to each other, then all to Christ.

These are the actions and meditations of the truly pious person: while the vulgar place all their religion in crowding up close to the altar, in listening to the words of the priest, and in being very circumspect at the observance of each trifling ceremony. Nor is it in such cases only as we have here given for instances, but through his whole course of life, that the pious man, without any regard to the baser materials of the body, spends himself wholly in a fixed intentness upon spiritual, invisible, and eternal objects.

Now since these persons stand off, and keep at so wide a distance between themselves, it is customary for them both to think each other mad: and were I to give my opinion to which of the two the name does most properly belong, I should, I confess, adjudge it to the religious; of the reasonableness whereof you may be farther convinced if I proceed to demonstrate what I formerly hinted at, namely, that that ultimate happiness which religion proposes is no other than some sort of madness.

First, therefore, Plato dreamed somewhat of this nature when he tells us that the madness of lovers was of all other dispositions of the body most desirable; for he who is once thoroughly smitten with this passion, lives no longer within himself, but has removed his soul to the same place where he has settled his affections, and loses himself to find the object he so much dotes upon: this straying now, and wandering of a soul from its own mansion, what is it better than a plain transport of madness? What else can be the meaning of those proverbial phrases, *non est apud se*, he is not himself; *ad te redi*, recover yourself; and *sibi redditus est*, he is come again to himself? And accordingly as love is more hot and eager, so is the madness thence ensuing more incurable, and yet more happy. Now what shall be that future happiness of glorified saints, which pious souls here on earth so earnestly groan for, but only that the spirit, as the more potent and prevalent victor, shall over-master and swallow up the body; and that the more easily, because while here below, the several members, by being mortified, and kept in subjection, were the better prepared for this separating change; and afterward the spirit itself shall be lost, and drowned in the abyss of beatific vision, so as the whole man will be then perfectly beyond all its own bounds, and be no otherwise happy than as transported into ecstasy and wonder, it feels some unspeakable influence from that omnipotent Being, which makes all things completely blessed, by assimilating them to his own likeness. Now although this happiness be then only consummated, when souls at the general resurrection shall be reunited to their bodies, and both be clothed with immortality; yet because a religious life is but a continued meditation upon, and as it were a transcript of the joys of heaven, therefore to such persons there is allowed some relish and foretaste of that pleasure here, which is to be their reward hereafter. And although this indeed be but a small pittance of satisfaction compared with that future inexhaustible fountain of blessedness, yet does it abundantly overbalance all worldly delights, were they all in conjunction set off to their best advantage; so great is the precedency of spiritual things before corporeal, of invisible before material and visible. This is what the apostle gives an eloquent

The Anticipation of Future Happiness.

description of, where he says by way of encouragement, that *eye hath not
seen, nor ear heard, nor hath it entered into the heart of man to conceive those things
which God hath prepared for them that love him.* This likewise is that better part
which Mary chose, which shall not be taken from her, but perfected and
completed by her mortal putting on immortality.

Now those who are thus devoutly affected (though few there are so),
undergo somewhat of strange alteration, which very nearly approaches to
madness; they speak many things at an abrupt and incoherent rate, as if
they were actuated by some possessing demon; they make an inarticulate
noise, without any distinguishable sense or meaning; they sometimes screw
and distort their faces to uncouth and antic looks; at one time beyond
measure cheerful, then as immoderately sullen; now sobbing, then laughing, and soon after sighing, as if they were perfectly distracted, and out of
their senses. If they have any sober intervals of coming to themselves again,
like St. Paul they then confess, that *they were caught up they know not where,
whether in the body, or out of the body, they cannot tell;* as if they had been in a
dead sleep or trance, they remember nothing of what they have heard,
seen, said, or done: this they only know, that their past delusion was a most
desirable happiness; that therefore they bewail nothing more than the loss
of it, nor wish for any greater joy than the quick return of it, and more
durable abode forever. And this (as I have said) is the foretaste or anticipation of future blessedness.

But I doubt I have forgot myself, and have already transgressed the
bounds of modesty. However, if I have said anything too confidently or
impertinently, be pleased to consider that it was spoke by Folly, and that
under the person of a woman; yet at the same time remember the applic-
ableness of that Greek proverb:

A fool oft speaks a seasonable truth:

Unless you will be so witty as to object that this makes no apology for me,
because the word ἀνὴρ signifies a man, not a woman, and consequently
my sex debars me from the benefit of that observation.

I perceive now, that, for a concluding treat, you expect a formal epilogue,
and the summing up of all in a brief recitation; but I will assure you, you are
grossly mistaken if you suppose that after such a hodgepodge medley of
speech I should be able to recollect anything I have delivered. Beside,
as it is an old proverb, μισῶ μνάμονα συμπόταν: *I hate a pot-companion with*

a good memory; so indeed I may as truly say, *μισψνάμοναν ἀκροατήν. I hate a hearer that will carry anything away with him.* Wherefore, in short:

Farewell! Live long, drink deep, be jolly,
Ye most illustrious votaries of folly!

A Poem on the Foregoing Work

THERE'S NE'ER A BLADE OF HONOUR IN THE TOWN,
    But if you chance to term him *fool* and *clown*,
Straight *satisfaction* cries, and then with speed
The time, the place, and rapier's length's decreed.
Prodigious fops, I'll swear, which can't agree
To be call'd what's their happiness to be:
    Blest *Idiots!*
That in an humble sphere securely move,
And there the sweets of a safe *dulness* prove,
Nor envy the proud heights of those who range above.
Folly, sure friend of a misguided will,
Affords a kind excuse for doing ill;
And *Socrates*, that prudent, thinking tool,
Had the gods lik'd him would have prov'd a *fool*.
Methinks our author, when without a flaw,
The graces of his mistress he does draw,
Wishes (if *Metempsychosis* be true,
And souls do change their case, and act anew),
In his next life he only might aspire
To the few brains of some soft country squire,
Whose head with such like rudiments is fraught,
As in his youth his careful grannum taught.

    And now (dear friend) how shall we to thy brow
Pay all those laurels which we justly owe?
For thou fresh honours to the work dost bring,
And to the theme: nor seems that pleasing thing,

Which he so well in *Latin* has express'd,
Less comical in *English* garments dress'd;
Thy sentences are all so clearly wrought,
And so exactly plac'd in every thought,
That, which is more oblig'd we scarce can see
The subject by thine author, or himself by thee.

FINIS

SUGGESTED READING

AUGUSTIJN, C. *Erasmus: His Life, Work and Influence.* Toronto: Toronto University Press, 1991.

BAINTON, ROLAND. *Erasmus of Rotterdam.* New York: Scribners, 1969.

BOYLE, MARJORIE O'ROURKE. *Christening Pagan Mysteries: Erasmus in Pursuit of Wisdom.* Toronto: Toronto University Press, 1982.

DEMOLEN, RICHARD L., ED. *Essays on the Works of Erasmus.* New Haven: Yale University Press, 1978.

EISENSTEIN, ELIZABETH. *The Printing Press as an Agent of Change.* Cambridge: Cambridge University Press, 1980.

ERASMUS, DESIDERIUS. *The Adages of Erasmus.* Trans. William Barker. Toronto: Toronto University Press, 2002.

——. *The Erasmus Reader.* Ed. Erika Rummel. Toronto: Toronto University Press, 1990.

HALE, JOHN. *The Civilization of Europe in the Renaissance.* New York: Antheneum, 1994.

HILLERBRAND, HANS J. *Erasmus and His Age.* New York: Harper & Row, 1970.

HUIZINGA, JOHAN. *Erasmus of Rotterdam.* London: Phaidon, 1952.

——. *The Autumn of the Middle Ages.* Trans. Rodney J. Payton and Ulrich Mammitzch. Chicago: Chicago University Press, 1996.

JARDINE, LISA. *Erasmus, Man of Letters: The Construction of Charisma in Print.* Princeton: Princeton University Press, 1993.

KAISER, WALTER JACOB. *Praisers of Folly: Erasmus, Rabelais, Shakespeare.* Cambridge: Cambridge University Press, 1963.

MCCONICA, JAMES. *Erasmus.* Oxford: Oxford University Press, 1991.

OBERMAN, HEIKO. *The Harvest of Late Medieval Theology.* Cambridge, MA: Harvard University Press, 1963.

PHILLIPS, MARGARET MANN. *Erasmus and the Northern Renaissance.* Woodbridge, Suffolk: Boydell, 1981.

SOWARDS, J. KELLY. *Desiderius Erasmus.* Boston: Twayne, 1975.

TRACY, JAMES D. *Erasmus of the Low Countries.* Berkeley, CA: University of California, 1996.

TREVOR-ROPER, HUGH. *Men and Events: Historical Essays.* New York: Hippocrene, 1977.

WILLIAMS, KATHLEEN, ED. *Twentieth Century Interpretations of The Praise of Folly.* Englewood Cliffs, NJ: Prentice-Hall, 1969.